Attack the Casino's Vulnerable Games!

John Gollehon
The Confident Gambler™

GOLLEHON BOOKS™
GRAND RAPIDS, MICHIGAN

MANUFACTURED IN THE UNITED STATES OF AMERICA

Library of Congress Catalog Card Number 2006930529

ISBN 0-914839-80-2
(International Standard Book Number)

GOLLEHON, THE CONFIDENT GAMBLER, and POWER
PROGRESSIVE STRATEGY are exclusive trademarks of
Gollehon Press, Inc.

Attack the Casino's Vulnerable Games incorporates revised and
expanded text from *Gambling's Winning Secrets* and text from
the author's earlier works including *Power Gambling*.

GOLLEHON BOOKS are published by: Gollehon Press, Inc.,
6157 28th St. SE, Grand Rapids, MI 49546.

GOLLEHON BOOKS are available in quantity purchases;
contact Special Sales. Gollehon does not accept unsolicited
manuscripts. Brief book proposals are reviewed.

Contents

1. Breaking The Casino's Code 1

2. Blackjack 15

3. Craps 58

4. Power Progressive Strategy 102

5. Video Poker 135

6. Texas Hold 'em 163

7. A Winner's Notebook 225

From The Author...

The decision to gamble is a personal one. It should take into account many things, not the least of which is your ability to wisely manage money. If you frequently overdraw your checking account, exceed your credit-card limits, or otherwise spend your money recklessly—buying on impulse, for example—suffice it to say, gambling is a bad idea.

If you do decide to try your luck, promise yourself that you will stay within your means. Gambling can be fun. Don't let serious losses take your fun away.

John Gollehon

Gaming Books Authored
By John Gollehon

Casino Games
Casino Gambling
Texas Hold 'em Take The Money!
Commando Craps & Blackjack!
Conquering Casino Craps
How To Win!
What Casinos Don't Want You To Know
Gambler's Edge

The All About Series:
All About Blackjack
All About Craps
All About Slots And Video Poker

Fun Facts Books:
Casino Fun Facts
Las Vegas Fun Facts
The Ultimate Winner's Guide to Gambling

*To gamblers
who mean business!*

CHAPTER 1

BREAKING THE CASINO'S CODE

Listen to me. I want you to win. I want to *help* you win! OK? I'm serious. There are few things I enjoy more than seeing players walk away from a table with chips falling out of their pockets. I like winners. I like to play with winners. I immerse myself in a winning frame of mind every minute I'm in action. You should do the same.

And you can call it whatever you want to. Positive thinking. Confidence. There are probably a thousand ways to say it, but only one way to pull it off. To win! And to win again!

For those of you who have read me before, you know how I feel about the conditioning of a player. Casinos have lots of ways of "conditioning" you. Conditioning you to lose, of course. But we can counter that effort, and we will, as we progress along. You'll learn how to play the "vulnerable" games—the smart games—make the right bets, and the right moves. But let's be frank. Any good gaming author can do that for you—teach you how to play. In my books, though, I like to go one step further. I want to teach you how to win! What a difference it can make when you have the confidence to attack the casino!

Incidentally, I chose that strong verb for the book's title for a reason. Other verbs could have worked: beat the casino, defeat the casino, and so on. But I like "attack!" I like it because it suggests the right kind of conditioning you should be in the next time you're in the trenches.

BE ALERT: To what, you ask? To changing trends. Good players can spot opportunities. Streaks of wins, dealer busts, players flush with chips, even a generally favorable climate to play in. Sometimes that's all you need. But you must search it out. Don't just plop yourself down and start playing. You are, after all, on a "search and attack" mission when you first play *and* every time you reboot a new session.

A key part of the casino's code is to encourage you to play. That's right, for longer than you probably intended, and perhaps at betting minimums that are higher than you wanted. They employ the most effective marketing tools imaginable to keep you at the tables (or the machines). Break that code by limiting your play to only those times when you're winning. If you're not winning, take a break. As you'll learn in a later chapter, a couple of bad pops in a row and I walk. If a casino beats me with a one-two punch, it won't get a third shot. It's Break City for me as I regroup and plan my next session.

BE SERIOUS: I recall watching a group of young players—early twenties, maybe— laughing it up pretty well as they exited a blackjack table. I figured they all won soundly, but as I overheard their conversation, I found out that wasn't the case at all. They had all been *beaten* soundly. And, apparently, it was funny.

If you can explain to me what's funny about losing, I'm listening. You take it in stride, but you should feel it in the pit of your stomach, just as I do. And the only way to counter the effects of that loss is with a win. If you take anything from this chapter, take this: Wins counter losses. You can't laugh them away any more than you can laugh those lost hundreds back into your wallet. Get serious!

All of this, incidentally, has nothing to do with your betting level. Big bettor, small bettor, makes no difference. If you're not serious about winning, I assure you… you won't.

You see, the entire ambiance of a casino is designed to put you in a fun mood, relaxed and off-guard. The casino wants you to think that you're there to have fun, laugh it up, let loose, and forget what you're really there for. Don't become a victim of its clever code. If you're not there to win money… *serious* money, then you have no business being there in the first place. Why blow your hard-earned paycheck on what really *isn't* fun anyhow? Gambling, my dear friend, has two components: winning and losing. Guess which one is the *real* fun.

BE SMART: I watched this same bunch wander over to the keno lounge as they counted what little money they had left. They were not only running out of money, they were running out of clues. What should they be doing? What shouldn't they do?

They played the game with no knowledge of percentages. It's obvious, or they wouldn't have played at all. Plainly said, keno is an expensive proposition. Sure, some dweeb will come along and hit 8 out of 8 spots for $50,000 and think he's the smartest gambler in town. Smart? Hardly. Lucky? You bet.

I can only hope that such a lucky player has the smarts to take it home and stuff it away… in a bank fund, investment account, stocks, bonds, something, anything! Anything but another shot at the casino, because the casino will get it back. All of it. Why? Because chief among the casino's code are percentages. Casinos rely on their "PC" to keep them in the game 24/7. It's why casino managers sleep so well at night. They know they have the percentages on their side. And they also know that players who knock down high-percentage wins almost always come back for more. And they get what's coming to them. They lose it ten times faster than they won it! And they're *not* laughing!

Smart players, on the other hand, are very familiar with percentages, and they fight the lowest they can find. In some cases, they don't have to fight. They've found percentages that might actually tip to their favor! Or they might find a game that has no percentages at all! That's right, they have only the skill of other players to contend with.

It's always surprised me how many players know little about the different bets scattered among the casino games, and the varying percentages offered. When you're shopping for a car, are you looking for a good deal or a bad deal? So why is "shopping" in a casino any different? Think about it.

A CRASH COURSE IN PERCENTAGES

I'm not going to overly complicate this for you. Here's all you really need to know about casino games that are based on house percentages: If the casino pays off your winning wager at something less than the true odds (likelihood) of winning that bet, it has acquired an advantage over you. And the actual percentage it keeps depends on how much or how little it underpays you.

In the chapter on craps, we'll talk more about this because craps is a game with lots of bets and lots of different percentages. But for now, let's list all the games—not just the smart ones—and the corresponding percentages. You'll quickly see which games (and which bets) are the good deals and the bad deals.

GAME	PERCENTAGE

BACCARAT   **1.13**

Percentage is averaged over number of player-hands (1.24%) and banker-hands (1.06%) played based on casino studies. Banker-hand is inclusive of commissions. Clearly, the banker-hand is the wiser choice. Does not reflect tie bets (14%).

BLACKJACK   **0.2 to 0.5**

Variations in game rules prevent listing of specific percentages. Always shop for the best playing conditions: blackjack pays 3 to 2, dealer must stand on all 17s, double down on any two cards, double after split, re-split aces. Multiple-decks increase percentage. Perfect basic strategy assumed. Professional-level card-counting can produce an infrequent player advantage.

CARIBBEAN STUD POKER   **5.23**

Progressive jackpot bets increase percentage.

CRAPS   0.2 to 16.67

This game has the widest spread of percentages among 25 different bets. The best bet is the odds-bet taken when a point-number is established on the pass-line or come. Singularly, the bet is fair, no house advantage, but it can only be made with a pass-line or come bet. Single odds effectively lowers the 1.41% house advantage for the pass-line or come bet to 0.83%. Double odds reduces it further to 0.61%. Triple odds, five-times odds, and ten-times odds (0.2%) are the better "multiple odds" offered by some casinos.

KENO   25 to 60

New variations in this game have produced bets with percentages over 60%! Typical percentages vary from 25% to 35%, steep by any standards. The game offers high jackpots for modest bets. But, virtually all low-risk, high-reward bets offered by casinos are costly in percentage terms.

LET IT RIDE   3.52

This game has always struck me as more difficult to beat than the percentage would indicate. Tread lightly.

3-CARD POKER   2.33 to 7.25

The same caveat applies. Among the newer poker-based games, this one has attracted more players, especially those who like to play a system. Many players push up the percentages.

PAI-GOW   3.0

Popular among Asians, but increasingly hard to find. Who cares?

REEL-TYPE SLOTS   2 to 20 and up

In general terms, the higher the coin denomination, the lower the percentage. Accordingly, players expect the lowest percentages on "high roller" slots. But do they get them? Who knows? In fact, all machines hide their percentages within the computer circuitry.

ROULETTE   1.35 to 5.26

Don't let the low 1.35% fool you. You'll only find it in few casinos (mostly European) offering "surrender" or "en prison" on even-money wagers on "single zero" wheels. The great majority of wheels in the United States are "double zero" meaning there are 38 compartments where the ball might land: 18 red numbers, 18 black numbers, and 2 green numbers. Since payoffs are based on 36 numbers, the 2 green numbers create the house advantage of 5.26% (1/19).

VIDEO POKER   0.6 to 8.5

The only "slot machine" that reveals its percentage based on the paytable, primarily the payouts for a flush and full house. The best machines pay out 7 coins for a flush and 10 coins for a full house (7-10). Most commonly found are 5-6, 5-8, and 6-9 machines. Be sure two pair pays two coins. Jacks-or-better must return your bet.

THE PLAYER'S CODE

Before we start discussion on all the "vulnerable" games to attack, we need to look in the mirror for a moment. My mention earlier of those incompetent players certainly was not indicative of the way *you* play, right? Of course not. But there are faults that even the most seasoned players have and don't realize it. The casinos don't even need to factor them in to their winning code. They have enough going for them already; this is no time for largess.

Other gaming writers will argue with my notion that a good player can exercise some control over the effects of percentages—control, both good and bad. Here's how I see it.

To the extent that game percentages contribute to the outcome—a winning or losing session—so can another kind of control: *self*-control. And there are times when I believe that your own control is more important than the control of percentages, especially in the short term, especially when the percentages are quite small. You should know that even small percentages can bite you in the long term, but let's talk short-term for a moment. In the short term, you can just about throw out the percentages because just about anything can happen. Including good things. Many good things. Unless you screw them up. Case in point.

My buddy, Phil, just got back from a small tribal casino in Northern Michigan, and I was expecting his call to tell me how he did. But Phil never called. Somewhat worried about him (he's not the healthiest gambler on the planet), I called his home and got his wife. Turns out that she was up there with him, too. And, with Phil resting from a rough trip, Nancy was anxious to fill me in. From the sound of her voice, I could tell it didn't go well.

Phil is a craps player like I am. We used to make a great team. We both played easy at first and got aggressive when the table heated up. Yeah, I know. Basic stuff. But Phil changed the rules, so I stopped playing with him. He'd go crazy on me.

Anyhow, here's how the conversation went down:

"John, you know Phil, he wanted to play craps so badly and they only had one table open. And what's worse, there were no players! It drove him nuts. He never wants to play at a dice table by himself. You don't, either, right?"

"Nope."

"So, all the way up there, a dice crew ready to go, and no players."

"Got it, Nancy."

"Well, I talked Phil into playing video poker with me. Within minutes, he hits a straight flush. Boy, did he get excited!"

"Good. But I know Phil. I can't imagine him sitting at a poker machine. He hates slots, you know."

"Oh yeah. Anyhow, another half-hour or so of pushin' buttons, and bang! He hit the big one!"

"A Royal flush?! Is that what you're telling me?!"

"Yep. The biggie. And he was on top of the world!"

"I would imagine. I've gotta razz him about that when I see him."

"No! Don't!"

"Why not?"

"Well, he got paid for the royal... in hundreds, ten hundred-dollar bills. Plus he had some winnings left from his earlier hits. And he says to me, 'Nancy, I'm gonna go over and see if they've got any dice players, yet.'"

"Uh-oh."

"You're right. I wanted to head home. He wanted to make one last walk past the tables. And it hadn't changed. No players. So he says to the crew, 'Gimme the dice. I'll start the game for you. I've got a little ammo here I didn't expect.'"

"Hmm."

"John, I'm so mad at him. He left every last dollar on that dice table. All of his winnings."

"Well, like I said, I know Phil. He wanted to play craps. Loves to play craps. Obviously, winning wasn't his objective. He had already accomplished that."

"It ruined our trip, John. This all happened on the day we were leaving for home."

"Yep. I understand."

"So, any advice, Mr. Expert?"

"Well, I know a good divorce attorney."

"Seriously."

"Tell him he has to change his focus. He has to focus on winning, not playing. But I've already told him that a thousand times. Holding on to a win has always been a problem for him. Even if his big win would have come at the craps table instead, he still might have given it back. Like I said, I know Phil. And I don't think Phil is going to change."

Dear readers: I don't like to end a chapter on a downer note, but I'm including this story because I believe that it might help some of you. I'll work on Phil, you work on yourself.

Discipline, my friends, Discipline with a capital D. Of all the strategies you are about to learn, none is more important than self-control.

CHAPTER 2

BLACKJACK

What was once the casino's signature game, blackjack has gone through considerable changes over the years. Casino bosses, even today, can't seem to keep their hands out of the tool box. Someone has to tell them that the wagon ain't broke, so stop trying to fix it!

It's important that you understand the game as it's played today, and not be misled by the attraction of the game's earlier features, which have gone the way of the 99-cent breakfast! OK, maybe you can still find a cheap breakfast somewhere, but if you want to play "pure" blackjack, you'll need a time machine set for the '60s. (Yeah, Baby!)

What's equally important to know is that today's game still can be beaten, still sports a low percentage, and can even swing to a negative percentage (in the players' favor) if you use the right strategy. Don't fear! You'll find the "right strategy" a bit later on in this chapter.

You'll also have some traps to avoid, such as continuous shuffling machines, which take all the fun out of card-counting. And you'll need to shop for the best playing conditions you can find. As an example, some casinos today have cut the payoff for a player blackjack from 3 to 2 to a lowly 6 to 5. And you thought only players were greedy?!

Before we delve into the secrets to beating this ever-changing game, let's be sure you understand the rules you'll most likely find in casinos today, and confirm the right player options to exercise. A concise rundown certainly won't hurt you.

HOW TO PLAY THE GAME

Standard-issue playing cards (with jokers removed) are dealt from a shoe (a box containing four or more decks) or by hand (usually one or two decks) to each player and the dealer, each getting two cards. One of the dealer's cards is face-up for everyone to see, while the other card is face-down.

The number-cards count as face-value, the "picture" cards count as 10, and the ace is counted as either 1 or 11, whichever is better to make or approach 21. The four suits have no significance.

The idea is to "beat the dealer" by either holding a hand that's closer to 21 than the dealer's hand (neither hand can exceed 21) or holding any hand while the dealer exceeds 21 by drawing additional cards. The strategy for playing your hand in an optimum fashion will be clearly spelled out for you in the following pages.

You may ask for an additional card, or as many as you like until you "stand" (are finished). If you take too many cards and exceed 21, it's an automatic "bust," and you immediately lose. Toss your cards on the table between the betting area and the dealer, indicating the bust. The dealer will remove your wager. **In most casinos today, all the player's cards are dealt face-up; you never need to touch the cards, and shouldn't.** In this case, when you bust, the dealer will remove your cards (and your wager) for you.

When all players at the table have acted on their hands, the dealer turns over the card dealt face-down (hole-card) and stands only if the total is 17 or more. The dealer is required to draw cards until the hand totals at least 17 or more. If the dealer busts in the process, all players who did not bust are automatic and immediate winners.

If, however, the dealer does not bust and has a hand that totals between 17 and 21 (which it must, because the dealer draws to make at least 17, and more than 21 is a bust) the hand is compared to yours to see which is closer to 21. Whichever is closer, wins. If both you and the dealer have the same total, it's called a "push" (a tie) and there's no decision on the bet. In that case, you are free to remove the wager, increase it, or decrease it. Only after a push, or after a win, can you again touch the chips in your betting area.

Never touch your bet after a game has begun and before the hand is settled. Casino personnel are very suspicious.

Now, read this brief section again carefully until you fully understand it. It's the essence of the game! If you're wondering on what hand-totals to draw cards, or at what point to stop drawing, don't worry about it now. We'll cover that later, at precisely the right time, for all possible hand combinations.

All bets that win are paid at even money. If you bet $5, you win $5, and so on. However, **if your first two cards are a 10-value card and an ace, it's called a "Blackjack" (wins outright) and *should be* paid at 3 to 2.** If you bet $10, you'll receive $15 in winnings! *The 10-value card does not need to be a picture-card.* A 10 of spades or any other suit is worth just as much as a jack, queen, or king. Any 10-value card and an ace make a blackjack.

If the dealer receives a blackjack on the first two cards, you lose at even money (only the amount of your wager) unless you also have a blackjack, in which case it's a push.

The only other exception to the even-money wagers is called "insurance." Here's how it works: If the dealer's up-card is an ace, the dealer will ask all the players if they wish to take insurance. To do that, you bet an additional amount up to one-half of your original wager, betting that the dealer does, in fact, have a 10-value card underneath, in which case your side-bet wins at 2 to 1 odds.

The bottom line on insurance is *don't do it!* It's a silly bet that only increases the house percentage.

HIT OR STAND MOTIONS

To recap, the most important option you have is to either "hit" or "stand." Your way of indicating to the dealer that you wish to hit or stand depends on whether the cards are dealt face-up or face-down. Although virtually all casinos today deal the player's cards face-up, a few casinos still deal the player's first two cards face-down, as was common many years ago. So, I'll cover both scenarios.

At tables where the cards are dealt face-up, you should never touch the cards. To signal a hit, you can make either of two motions:

I prefer to point at the cards, actually touching the table with my finger about two to three inches from the cards. This way, there's no question that I want another card. Unfortunately, some casinos frown on this action for whatever illogical reason.

The other motion is to simply bring your hand toward you in a scooping motion. But be sure you do this over the table, so the "eye in the sky" can see it to record. (The casino's video cameras are there to protect both the casino and the player. Don't be intimidated by them. Every table is in fine focus.)

If you don't want another card, I recommend that you simply put out your hand, toward the dealer, as if to indicate "stop." The casino recommends a horizontal motion as if you're wiping a piece of glass above the table.

However, it's been my experience that the latter motion can easily be confused with the opposite signal, especially if a player is particularly sloppy with the motions. Try my way.

At tables where the cards are dealt face-down, you obviously must pick up the cards to read your hand. If you do not want another card, simply place both cards face-down on the table and slightly under your bet. In most casinos, it's all right to simply place the cards within close proximity of your wager.

If you want a hit, keep the cards in your hand until it's your turn to play. Then, lightly scrape the card edges on the table, toward you.

Incidentally, it makes no difference whether the cards are dealt face-down or face-up in blackjack. This isn't poker! But, it does make a significant difference to card-counting that we'll discuss later.

SPLITTING

Another important option for you is to "split" identical cards in your original hand, such as a pair of 8s. When this option is available, you do not just automatically do it! The decision to split or not to split your pair depends on whether or not it will be an advantage to you.

When we get to our "basic strategy" later on, I'll detail each possible pair combination in comparison to the dealer's up-card, and tell you the optimum decision you should make.

For now, however, let's prematurely make two important rules abundantly clear: **Never, never, never split 10-value cards, such as two face-cards, and never split 5s and 4s. Always split aces and 8s!** If you're an inexperienced player, see if you can quickly understand the solid reasoning behind these two important rules.*

When you wish to split your cards at a face-down table, simply position your cards face-up and behind your bet (to the dealer's side). Then,

---

*Splitting 10-value cards is my favorite example of greed. You're throwing away an excellent hand! Players who split a 20 should have their heads examined.

make another wager of the same size and place it directly beside (not on top of) your original bet. At a face-up table, you only need to make a new bet inside the betting circle to indicate the split, since your cards are already in position.

Tell the dealer you wish to split the pair, and you will be given two more cards, one to each card you split, creating two new hands that are working for you. If you receive another identical card, some casinos will allow you to split again, and you'll have three hands in play.

However, most casinos today do not allow the re-splitting of aces. To make matters worse, the hands stand after the dealer has given one card to each of the split aces. The casino will not afford you the option of hitting. Regardless, **splitting aces is a strong player advantage. Always do it.**

DOUBLE DOWN

Here's an option that figures significantly in your ability to adjust the percentages. You may "double down" on your first two cards by making an additional bet up to the amount of your original wager and receive only one card from the dealer. One hit.

Obviously, the time to double down is when you have a hand-total of 10 or 11 and the dealer's up-card is 6 or less. That's the ideal situation. Another 10-value card will give you a 20 or 21. Even a 7, 8, or 9 will give you a pat hand (17 or better). That's the reason I told you earlier never to split 5s. The two 5-value cards give you a hand-total of 10, and that's usually a good time to double down.

I'll give you the complete basic strategy for doubling down, and all the other player options, later on. You'll know exactly when to do it, and when not to.

As I've mentioned before, the casino industry has been negligent in its efforts to standardize game rules. Perhaps it's an element of competition that shouldn't be standardized. Just remember that the rules do vary, and doubling down is a good example.

Some casinos limit doubling down to only 10 or 11. Still other casinos will allow doubling down on any two cards, and that's a big advantage to the player, as you'll learn later.

Unfortunately, most casinos not only have different rules, they change their rules about as often as your gas bill goes up. So, the best solution is to simply ask before you play.

SURRENDER

"Surrender" is an option that few players understand or readily use. Probably because many casinos no longer offer it. If you are fortunate to play in a casino where it is available, this is what it means to you: If you don't like your first two cards, and that happens a lot, you can surrender the hand and lose only one-half of your bet.

To surrender, simply state "surrender" to the dealer and throw in your cards. The dealer will remove half of your bet, and you're out of the woods. It's that simple.

There was a time when I refused to play blackjack in any casino without surrender rules. Who wants to hit a 15 or 16 against the dealer's 10? Years ago, a player could surrender before the peek! It was called "early surrender," and casinos promoted it wildly to attract players. The rule was rather rudely downgraded in later years to "late surrender," where a player could only surrender *after* the peek. Suffice it to say, casinos today are getting all the players they need... without it.

A SOFT HAND

Any hand that includes an ace has two values… a soft value and a hard value. If your hand is an ace-6, the soft value is 17 (counting the ace as 11), the hard value is 7 (counting the ace as 1).

Although it doesn't come up that often, there's a decision to make whether or not to hit a soft 17 or 18. A soft 19 or 20 is good enough and you should stand. But it's important to remember that a soft hand, such as a soft 17, will not bust. A 10-value card will simply make the soft 17 hard. Depending on the dealer's up-card, you actually may want to double down on a soft 17, if the casino allows you to do it. I'll give you the basic strategy for soft hands in the following pages.

Earlier in this chapter, I told you that the dealer is required to draw to 16 and stand on 17. That's the basic rule on the Strip in Las Vegas and in most other major casinos across the country. But in much of Northern Nevada, downtown Las Vegas, and some Indian casinos, the rule is different, requiring the dealer to hit a soft 17. It's a nasty ploy, and definitely a disadvantage to the player.

Look on the table layout before you play. It should clearly state, "The dealer must draw to 16 and stand on *all* 17s." Much better!

BASIC STRATEGY

Before we look at the charts, let's apply some good old-fashioned "horse-sense" and see if we can understand the reasoning behind the strategies. You'll be able to remember these strategies more easily if you understand why they work!

First, let's identify the potential bust hands as "stiffs." And it's a great term for them. When the dealer gives you a hard, unpaired 12, 13, 14, 15, or 16, you got stiffed! If your hand is 15 or 16 (other than 8-8), you've got one of the two worst hands possible and especially tough if the dealer's up-card is a 7 or higher.

Don't screw it up any more than it already is by not hitting it, or by not surrendering it if you can.

If your cards total 17, 18, 19, or 20, it's a "pat" hand. It's decent. Although 17 and 18 may be good enough to stand on, they certainly won't get all the marbles all the time. 19s, 20s, and blackjacks are the real goodies you're looking for.

Judging by what we now understand to be the object of the game, and the basic game rules themselves, it would appear that the biggest casino advantage is the fact that the player has to draw before the dealer does.

That simple fact accounts for a hefty seven-percent advantage to the house.* So many inexperienced players, sensing that problem, elect to never hit a stiff for fear of busting. That dumb little ploy is worth about three percent to the house. We can work down the seven-percent advantage other ways, but not that way!

Now, see if you can identify the "good" cards and the "bad" cards for the player. It's important. Think about it.

It would seem obvious that all 10-value cards are good, because they help give you 20s, and pair

---

*Some casinos that offer a single-deck or double-deck game are now paying only 6 to 5 for a blackjack. Most casinos dealing six or eight decks have retained the 3-to-2 payoff. If you don't get 3 to 2, don't play! The 3-to-2 payoff reduces the house advantage from seven percent to a little under five percent.

Perfectly executed player options based on "basic strategy," including hitting, standing, doubling, and splitting for both hard and soft hands, will lower the house percentage to about ½ percent. This number cannot be determined precisely because of variations in rules.

up nicely with an ace for a blackjack. Sure, 10-value cards are good!

What about 2s, 3s, 4s, 5s, and 6s? They help to promote those lousy stiffs, right? And, more important, they can improve a dealer's stiff hand. 2s, 3s, 4s, 5s, and 6s are indeed bad cards!

Although we're getting a little ahead of ourselves, the object of card-counting is to determine how many 10-value cards and how many "small cards" are left in the deck, based on how many you've seen played.

When the ratio of 10-value cards to small cards is high, you have an advantage. If there are too many small cards left in the deck, the casino has a distinct advantage.

The strategies that follow are very powerful, but understand that no strategy will help you win if you don't help yourself.

Knowledge is power. But poor play on your part—reckless, senseless betting—can destroy that power in no time. Do yourself a favor. Read *What Casinos Don't Want You To Know*, a perfect complement to this book. The chapters on money management and common-sense betting will add a new, vital dimension to your game.

The most powerful strategies in the world are useless to you if you aren't disciplined. Discipline is still the most powerful strategy of all!

HIT-OR-STAND STRATEGY FOR STIFFS

PLAYER'S HARD HAND	DEALER'S UP-CARD									
	2	3	4	5	6	7	8	9	10	A
16	S	S	S	S	S	H	H	H	H	H
15	S	S	S	S	S	H	H	H	H	H
14	S	S	S	S	S	H	H	H	H	H
13	S	S	S	S	S	H	H	H	H	H
12	H	H	S	S	S	H	H	H	H	H

H=HIT   S=STAND

ALWAYS STAND ON 17 OR BETTER!

Our strategy for hitting or standing with stiffs is really quite simple, as you can see.

Always hit a stiff when the dealer has a 7 or higher. Remember it as 7-UP, and you'll never forget it.

Always stand on a stiff when the dealer has a 6 or less showing, with the exception of 12. The dealer does not have a pat hand (with the exception of ace-6) so there is a good possibility the dealer will bust.

Always stand on 17 or better. Never, even in your wildest dreams, hit 17! Dealers must alert pit bosses in many casinos when a player hits 17 or better. See if you can guess why.

Always draw a card on 11 or less. You might actually double down or split depending on the card values, but at the very least, you'll always hit it.

Incidentally, the hit-and-stand rules apply not only to your original hand, but to your hand at any time. For example, if your original hand is 10-4 against the dealer's 10, you hit it. You receive a 2. Now you have 16. According to the chart, you must continue hitting (until you have 17 or better).

Sure, the odds are against you, but you had a losing hand in the first place. **Over the long term, you'll reduce the casino's initial advantage we talked about by about 2.5 percent with correct hitting and standing strategy.** Reducing the percentages against you is the name of the game.

HARD DOUBLE-DOWN STRATEGY

PLAYER'S HARD HAND	DEALER'S UP-CARD									
	2	3	4	5	6	7	8	9	10	A
11	D	D	D	D	D	D	D	D	D	D
10	D	D	D	D	D	D	D	D	H	H
9	H	D	D	D	D	H	H	H	H	H

H=HIT   D=DOUBLE

Notice that you should always double down on 11, regardless of the dealer's up-card.

Doubling on 10 is restricted to a dealer's up-card of 9 or lower. If the dealer's up-card is 10 or an ace, it's obviously too risky.

Only double down on 9 if the dealer's up-card is 3, 4, 5, or 6. It's a moot point in many casinos where doubling is limited to 10 or 11. Doubling after you have split is equally restricted in many casinos. Ask before you play to be sure you understand the rules in a particular casino. Always seek out the best playing conditions.

Proper strategy for hard double downs (and for soft doubling that we'll cover under "Soft-Hand Strategy") further reduces the casino percentage by about 1.5 percent. We're getting there!

SPLITTING STRATEGY

PLAYER'S HAND	DEALER'S UP-CARD									
	2	3	4	5	6	7	8	9	10	A
A-A	SP	SP	SP	SP	SP	SP	SP	SP	SP	SP
10-10	S	S	S	S	S	S	S	S	S	S
9-9	SP	SP	SP	SP	SP	SP	SP	SP	S	S
8-8	SP	SP	SP	SP	SP	SP	SP	SP	SP	SP
7-7	SP	SP	SP	SP	SP	SP	H	H	H	H
6-6	SP	SP	SP	SP	SP	H	H	H	H	H
5-5	D	D	D	D	D	D	D	D	H	H
4-4	H	H	H	H	H	H	H	H	H	H
3-3	H	H	SP	SP	SP	SP	H	H	H	H
2-2	H	H	SP	SP	SP	SP	H	H	H	H

H=HIT   S=STAND   D=DOUBLE   SP=SPLIT

Always split aces and 8s. Never split 10s, 5s and 4s.

Treat 5-5 as 10 and follow our double-down rule—double if the dealer shows 9 or less, otherwise, just hit.

Split 9s when the dealer has 9 or less, split 7s when the dealer has 7 or less, and split 6s when the dealer has 6 or less. Remember that the dealer's up-card is always the same or less than the card you're splitting with 6s, 7s, and 9s.

Only split 3s and 2s when the dealer's up-card is 4, 5, 6, or 7. Otherwise, just hit.

SOFT-HAND STRATEGY

PLAYER'S SOFT HAND	DEALER'S UP-CARD									
	2	3	4	5	6	7	8	9	10	A
A-9 (20)	S	S	S	S	S	S	S	S	S	S
A-8 (19)	S	S	S	S	S	S	S	S	S	S
A-7 (18)	S	S	D	D	D	S	S	H	H	H
A-6 (17)	H	H	D	D	D	H	H	H	H	H
A-5 (16)	H	H	D	D	D	H	H	H	H	H
A-4 (15)	H	H	D	D	D	H	H	H	H	H
A-3 (14)	H	H	D	D	D	H	H	H	H	H
A-2 (13)	H	H	D	D	D	H	H	H	H	H

H=HIT S=STAND D=DOUBLE

Always stand on a soft 19 and 20. They represent good hands, regardless of the dealer's up-card.

Always double down (if it's allowed) on a soft 13 through 18 when the dealer has a 4, 5, or 6 showing. Otherwise hit 13 through 17.

A soft 18 is the most difficult to remember because there are three options. **Always double down on a soft 18 when the dealer is showing a 4, 5, or 6 (just like the smaller soft hands) and hit it when the dealer is showing a 9, 10, or ace.**

With a 9 or higher up-card, the dealer may have a better hand, so it does pay to try to improve your soft 18. Remember, you can't bust any soft hand with a single hit. However, if you end up with a poor draw, such as a 5, you must hit it again (hard 13) and take your chances.

SURRENDER STRATEGY

The rules for surrender are so simple that we don't need a graphic chart to show you.

PLAYER'S HAND	DEALER'S UP-CARD
15-16 (hard)	7-8-9-10-A

Surrender a 15 or 16 stiff (except 8-8) when the dealer has a 7 or higher up-card, if you're playing in a casino where it is allowed.

Surrender is worth nearly one percent to you, so look for it. But don't expect to find it in one-casino markets. This rule is generally offered as a casino marketing tool in competitive venues, assuming there are empty tables to fill.

Don't hesitate to lose half of your bet with a bad hand. It beats losing it all!

BASIC STRATEGY CARDS: A SMART WAY TO PLAY

As far as basic strategy is concerned, it's not as tough today to apply as it was years ago. To-day we have strategy cards for all the casino games (see ad on last page), which have been approved by nearly all casinos for players to use at the tables.

A blackjack basic strategy card shows every dealer up-card and player-hand combination. The card tells you what to do. There is no guesswork. The Gollehon strategy card for blackjack offers a great benefit to players in the sense that only one strategy card is needed for all the game variants, including the number of decks in play, from one deck to eight decks! Other cards on the market designated for a certain game variation may only serve to confuse most players, wondering if they've chosen the right card. With the Gollehon strategy card for blackjack, you always know you've got the right card!

It's best, obviously, to memorize the right moves, but let's be realistic. Some players are only occasional players. They can't be expected to remember all the player options and perform flawlessly during those twice-a-year trips to Vegas. For such players, strategy cards are a godsend. But I'm sure you're wondering why casinos allow their use. Simple. The cards speed up the games. There's no pondering. No hair-twirling. No looking up to the heavens for help. It's all right there in front of you. There's absolutely no reason to slow down the game. Yes, casinos love these cards. The more hands played, the more the casino makes. It's that simple.

I hope you didn't think that all you had to do was get your hands on a good basic strategy card and you could tell your boss what he could do with your crummy job. Not quite. As good as these cards are, they are not going to wipe out all the casinos. With the way the game is being played today in most venues, correct basic strategy will get the house percentage down to a little less than one-half percent. A nearly even game.

BEYOND THE BASICS

Blackjack is a "patience" game; the key is waiting for the right opportunities. But patience needs to come before you even sit down. Don't rush to play. The top players I know will watch a table, maybe several tables, for as long as it takes, before they decide to play. The term they like to use for this maneuver is called *drifting;* they are getting a drift for the tables.

Now let's talk about you for a moment. When you've finally found a spot, do you feel relieved, comfortable to get off your feet and settled in? Most players do. But that doesn't work, either!

Top players never think in terms of settling in. Never settled! Not by any stretch. It's an interesting dichotomy of discipline: The pro players have the patience to seek out what appears to be a "receptive table." But no patience at all if they are rudely welcomed. They are sitting on the edge of their chairs, fully prepared to escape quickly if the table turns into an ambush.

When I used to give talks on casino games, blackjack was always the game that drew the greater audiences. I would start each discussion by asking a question about table conditions. I would identify a condition that is increasingly becoming the standard fare, no matter the casino, no matter the venue: full tables, even on weekdays. The question would usually leave listeners stumped.

Here's what I would ask: "Let's say the casino is crowded; you want to play but all the tables are full. You've spotted a guy ready to leave a table because he just lost all of his money. But why would you want to take his place?"

The top players I know take the same stance about playing conditions as I do. If a dealer is particularly strong, for example, making pat hands out of stiffs and basically cleaning out the players, I see it as a trend, not an anomaly. Regardless of the game, seasoned players believe that trends are strangely stubborn and tend not to change in some remarkably quick fashion. Smart players go with the trends. Smart players would never sit themselves down at such a dangerous table.

Sure, there could be a sudden change in fortune. But what do you think? What do you think is more likely to happen? If you don't investigate before you play, you won't even know if there is a trend to monitor.

The first thing to do when you decide to play blackjack is not to play... for a while. Not until you've found a spot that seems safe. And if the casino is so busy that you can't really do any serious shopping of table conditions, you're in the wrong casino! Or you've picked a time to play when it's too busy.

Are you just going to wait it out, grab the first open chair and play? I hope not! I would like to think that this discussion has tempered your anxiety to play.

You're right. That's another advantage of table shopping. No one should play when they're in an anxious state, under the gun, and feeling pressure. Learn how to enjoy the time *before* you play. It should be a time of anticipation, not anxiety. Use it wisely.

Most players think that the essence of the game is to get to 21, or closer to 21 than the dealer. But that's not exactly true. In fact, it's a common misread right out of the starting

gate. **Far too many players simply misunderstand the workings of the game! The real essence of blackjack, dear friend, is simply to beat the dealer!**

Even if you win by doubling down on a soft 17, and end up making a mess of it, who cares? A win is a win! Do you think that someone takes points away from you because you won with a weak hand? Or gives you points because you boldly smacked a 16, even though you ended up doing a belly-flop? Hey, this isn't Olympic diving! There's no scoring to worry about. The idea is to win, regardless of how you get there.

Forget about "drawing to 21" or always making a pat hand, and take that fear of busting out of your head, too. Players who live by this misconception tend to make two critical mistakes.

First, some players tend to draw excessively to get that "closest to 21" hand. Even though they may know basic strategy, they chuck the charts and make up their own rules.

Second, some players take the opposite approach—not drawing when they should draw—relying too heavily on the dealer's likelihood of busting.

The key to at least having a chance at this game is to follow basic strategy to the letter. Never amend the strategy rules to suit your own misguided understanding of how the game is played. Basic strategy needs no special tweaking on your part; it has been proven to be the best approach to beating this game, and I mean "proven" over decades and decades of play.

The mathematical wizards who conquered this game in the 1960s—yes, that long ago—devised basic strategy with what is now time-tested accuracy. It's a testament to the work of these great pioneers of blackjack. You wouldn't dare mess with their work, would you? If you had a *little* misunderstanding, you've got it straight now, right? Good!

Then let's get on to the other aspect of beating blackjack—card counting. And for that, we again credit those elite mathematicians of yesteryear.

Boy! Talk about getting it right the first time! They were right on the money! To help you and generations of players WIN money!

It's an absolute given. You must count the cards if you want to have a chance to beat the game over the long term. And here's the good

news: **The card-counting strategy you use does not necessarily need to be complicated. There are easy ones. In fact, the strategy I'm about to give you is clearly the easiest *and* most effective. That's right. I'm going to give you your cake and you can eat it, too!**

Card-counting is the hallmark of any black-jack strategy. It's one of the few strategies that casinos actually fear. Knowing that played cards affect the distribution of future cards is the essence of card-counting.*

If there were strategy cards for counting cards, the casinos would not allow them. No chance. So don't bother looking for any. If you're going to do some fancy counting, you're going to have to do it in your head.

So why won't the casinos allow card-counting strategy cards? You can answer that one yourself. A good counter practicing basic strategy can literally take that minuscule percentage away from the casinos. Steal it right from under their noses. And then turn it against them. No, I don't think the casinos would be very receptive to that.

*Card-counting is obviously not effective on tables with continuous shuffling machines.

But don't let the idea of having to do all this counting stuff in your head scare you away. Here's another example where new strategies have been created, refined from older methods that were far too complicated anyhow.

THE IMPERIAL II COUNT STRATEGY

One of the neatest card-counting strategies is what I call the Imperial II Count. It's a modernization of one of my earliest strategies that was based on an overview of played cards. It seems almost too simple to work, but it does!

First, let me give you the basics behind the Imperial II Count so that you can understand the underlying principles. You'll be able to play it more efficiently if you understand how and why it works.

Most all casino blackjack tables today are played full, or nearly so. Years ago, you could always find an open table and play the dealer head-on. One on one. And many of the older strategies, such as my original Imperial Count, were designed for just that situation. But it's become increasingly difficult to have a one-on-one confrontation with a dealer today. Why? Well, we can look to the airlines for the answer. How many planes fly full today? The answer, I'm sure you'll agree, is all of them!

The casinos have decided to run their games with the same economics in mind. There are few, if any, open tables because open tables are not making money. On weekends, it's even tough to find open seats! Indeed. The casinos have wised up and, like the airlines, now force their customers to play musical chairs. It seems as if every time you look for a seat, there are three available and four players who want them.

So, for a card-counting strategy to be useful today, it must work at a full table of seven players. A perfect number for the Imperial II Count.

Another sign of the times is multiple-deck shoes. Outside of Nevada, your chances of finding a one- or two-deck game are slim and none, and slim just left town. There's no question about it, a good strategy today must be designed for multiple decks, particularly an eight-deck shoe. Eight decks is a perfect number for the Imperial II Count.

Virtually all multiple-deck games today are dealt with the cards face up. And that's an important consideration for card-counting. How can you count them if you can't see them?

Full tables, multiple decks, cards face up. So far, so good.

Knowing that the small cards—2, 3, 4, 5, and 6—are bad cards for players, keeping a count of these cards, and only these cards, is the center-piece of the Imperial II Count. The 10-value cards and the ace are the good cards for players, but we don't have to keep track of them because the Imperial II Count is a balanced count (five small-card values vs. five good-card values—A-K-Q-J-10). Keeping track of both good and bad cards would be redundant.

The more small cards that are removed from the shoe the better. Ideally, the small cards should leave the shoe at a higher than normal exit rate, and that's what the Imperial II Count does: It measures *the rate* at which the small cards are played.

To make the Imperial II Count work best for you, always position yourself at "third base," the seat at the far left of the table, so that you can see as many played cards as possible before you act on your hand. If there are seven players at the table, you will see an average of 21 cards per deal—including yours, all hits, and the dealer's up-card. Based on the ratio of small cards to all other cards, eight of these cards should be small ones.

Simply count these small cards as you see them. If you count ten after the first deal, there's a slight player advantage. If you count six, there's a slight additional edge for the casino.

There's one obvious glitch in this strategy that needs to be accounted for. The counting procedure I just outlined—looking for eight small cards out of a 21-card average—is based on the dealer's up-card being 7 or higher. If the dealer's up-card is one of the small cards you're tracking—2, 3, 4, 5, or 6—then you must adjust your card average downward, accounting for fewer player hits, with the net result that you will only be looking for seven small cards.*

If the table only has six players, you need to make another adjustment. With a dealer up-card of 7 or higher, look for seven small cards. If the

---

*Remember to count the dealer's small card, too. So you'll only be looking for six small cards among the players at a full table.

dealer's up-card is one of the small cards you're tracking, look for five more small cards.*

If the table has fewer than six players, avoid it. If the table where you're playing has six players and loses a player, move to another table with more players. Remember, you want as many players as possible in order to see as many cards as possible.

Imperial II Count Strategy

DEALER'S UP-CARD: 7 THRU ACE		DEALER'S UP-CARD: 2 THRU 6	
PLAYERS	SMALL CARDS	PLAYERS	SMALL CARDS
7	8	7	7
6	7	6	6

*The value of 21 cards per deal to seven hands is based on an average of 2.857 cards per hand when the dealer's up-card is 7 or higher, and 2.280 cards per hand when the dealer's up-card is 2 through 6. The values are based on actual casino studies. Computer models, based on perfect basic strategy and the widely used new standard for game rules, show these values to be somewhat higher. The deviations are most likely due to player-option errors resulting in lower hit frequencies. The numbers listed for "small cards" are simply the product of .3846 (small-card expectancy) and the cards-per-hand averages plus 1 (the dealer's up-card), times the number of players. The effects of rounded values should be negligible in the short term.

KEEPING THE COUNT

Perhaps the neatest feature of the Imperial II Count is the way you actually keep a record of the rate of small cards appearing. I recommend using a chip as your means of recording the results. Choose a part of the chip's artwork to act as an hour-hand, as if the chip is a clock face. Point the hand at 12 o'clock (straight up) to indicate a neutral count. As your count moves up in a favorable direction, simply turn the chip so that the hand is pointing to the right, perhaps at one o'clock. If the count is heading in a non-favorable direction, move the hand to the left.

The incremental turn of the chip is something you'll have to tweak for yourself. But it has to be relative to the degree with which you are seeing the small cards removed from the deck. Most of the time, you'll count the normal number of small cards for a particular deal, so you would not turn your chip.

I only turn the chip a full hour's worth, for example, when I see a deal with a significant fluctuation from the norm of, say, three or four cards. I've played this new version of the Imperial Count for about two years, and I've never been in a position where the hand was pointing past five o'clock. Since the right half of the chip is positive and the left half is negative, so to speak, you should not move the hand beyond six o'clock.

USING YOUR NEW SKILLS

Just keeping the count is one thing; using it is another. So how do you use it? It's easy. **Simply use your count to adjust the size of your wagers. Make larger wagers when the count is player-favorable, and, logically, smaller wagers when the count is running against you.** Again, I don't like making hard-and-fast rules about this, but the following chart should help you in structuring your wagers. But it should be used only as a guide.

NON-FAVORABLE			FAVORABLE		
COUNT	HAND	BET	COUNT	HAND	BET
0	NOON	TM	3	1 PM	2X
3	11 AM	TM	6	2 PM	3X
6	10 AM	EXIT	9	3 PM	5X

TM stands for Table Minimum. "Hand" refers to the hour locations on a clock face. The wager amounts are to show a bet-spread relationship only, and are not suggestive of specific dollar amounts. Wagers should never exceed the table minimum if values are not well within the right side of the clock. Change tables when the values have stagnated on the left side of the clock.

If you're relatively new to this game, you might have already realized the second advantage of card-counting. That's right. There are two. You now know that card-counting helps you by telling you when to bet more, when to bet less, and when not to bet at all. But did you know that it also helps you by telling you when to alter basic strategy? It's such an obvious feature, when you think about it, that we really don't need a chart to explain it. If, for example, you are dealt a 10-6—a likely bust-hand—and the dealer is showing 9, basic strategy says you should hit that stiff. Ideally, you would like to know that there is an excess of small-value cards remaining to be played. But what if your count indicates that there is actually a deficiency of small cards remaining? A deficiency of small cards most likely means an excess of 10-value cards. You certainly don't want a 10-value card in this case so you alter basic strategy and stand instead of hit.

Good card-counters, playing in ideal conditions, can detect those times when the edge has moved across the table. And for that fleeting moment, they've done something that other players at other games can't do: predict opportunity.

When I talked about sizing up blackjack tables at the top of this chapter, I didn't men-

tion the number of decks being played because you weren't ready for it then, but you are now. Look for the fewest decks being played. Eight decks are the worst, six decks are a little better, one-deck and two-deck games are the best.*

Most players think that the introduction of multiple-deck shoes to the blackjack scene was merely to cut down on the number of shuffles, thus giving the casinos more decisions per hour, which is what they want. I'm sure that was a factor, but it wasn't the overriding reason for this major change to the game.

Multiple decks of cards tend to smooth out fluctuations. In other words, more decks produce a more random distribution of cards. There is less likelihood that small cards, for example, will "clump" within the shoe.

Now you've got it. The changeover to multiple decks was just another strike against card-counting. A very effective one, indeed.**

*Single-deck and double-deck games are where you'll most likely find the short payoff for a blackjack. Remember: if you can't get a 3-to-2 payoff for a blackjack, don't play.

**The use of multiple decks takes away some of the advantages of both basic strategy and card-counting. A six-deck or eight-deck shoe can easily cost players half of a percent.

If you saw four aces removed from a one-deck game during the early deals, you can bet your bottom dollar that you won't see any more for the remainder of the deck. But if you saw four aces removed from an eight-deck shoe, the absence of those four aces, although significant, is far less significant.

The effects of early anomalies in an eight-deck shoe are clearly not as dramatic as the effects on a single or double deck.

It's all based on what mathematicians call *dilution*. The more cards to select from, the less likely certain cards will pair up. It explains the unusual drop in frequency of blackjacks, for example. Expect more from a single deck; expect less, proportionally, from an eight-deck shoe. Clearly, a multiple-deck game presents problems with or without continuous shufflers.

There's yet another contributor to this strange phenomenon. It's called *entropy*, a mathematical term that explains the tendency of objects to move away from their original order. It's best understood by visualizing a jar half-full of jelly beans with all the red ones on the bottom and the black ones on top. The more you shake the jar, the more "dispersed" the beans become.

You would never be able to reverse this disorder by further shaking. You wouldn't expect them to ever "reassemble" with the reds on the bottom and the black ones on top. But if we used only a few beans instead of half the jar, we *would* have a chance (although we might not have the time) to restore the original order.

And so it goes with the shoe games in casinos throughout the world. Today, casino bosses want to see lots and lots of cards on the blackjack tables, moving further and further away from order, through shuffle after shuffle.

That's right. The cards are continually moving toward chaos.

Chaos for the card-counter.

LOOKING AT THE BRIGHT SIDE

Sure, being a card-counter is not what it used to be. But that's not to say it isn't worth doing. Let me tell you how I play blackjack, what I look for, and what I settle for.

First and foremost, I can't play against a continuous shuffler. I want to count cards; in fact, I enjoy it. But a continuous shuffler makes the effort a waste of time. Incidentally, don't think that all shuffling machines are continuous. Many casinos use machines that shuffle a number of decks separate from the decks in play. That's different. That's OK.

Knowing it's nearly impossible for me to find a single-deck game with a full payoff for a black-jack—given the casino markets I'm close to—I give up the half percent for multiple decks instead of giving up nearly three times that figure for the short blackjack payoff at a hand-held game (one or two decks). I need full double-down privi-leges, and I need a reasonable cut-card penetra-tion. If more than one-and-one-half decks are cut out of an eight-deck shoe, I'll pass. Some casinos cut more than two full decks! To a card-counter, taking such a high percentage of cards out of play is a slap in the face!

There is a bright side to the issue of card dis-persion that we just talked about. As it relates to casino games, the *permeation* of cards is the term more popularly used, and it's not just at black-jack, but other card games as well—baccarat and even Texas Hold 'em, for example.

Is there a flip side to the "disorder" theory of mixing? Is there an inherent flaw in the hand-shuffling of cards? A poker player would ask if there's a predictable element to the selection of community cards, for example. If two aces are tossed into the pile together, might they stay together for the next deal?*

The question really is this: Just exactly how thorough is a good shuffling?

This novel question should not be taken lightly. Card values are clumped before the seal is broken on a new deck. The cards run in numerical order; the face cards, for example, are grouped together. When multiple decks are used, the dealers scoop up the cards in such a way that the face cards of one deck actually clump with another.

Test the theory yourself. Stack a deck with all four cards of any same value placed anywhere in the deck. Shuffle the heck out of them and see how they were dispersed. You might be *very* surprised.

---

*Without an interest in card-distribution anomalies, the seemingly never-ending list of casino-imposed drawbacks can take a player out of the game. In fact, today I play mostly Texas Hold 'em, and craps when I feel the anticipation, relegating blackjack to the back burner. But a recent study of deck-construction components has perked my interest, and I include this material here in the hope that it will perk yours, too.

In fact, experts who study the randomness of selection in casino games (the keno hopper and roulette wheel bias are the most mentioned examples), believe that a perfectly random shuffle is all but impossible. (The jury's still out on continuous shuffling machines.)

It's why I said earlier that I no longer mind going up against multiple decks at the blackjack tables as much as I do many of the other casino countermeasures.

I've fought tougher battles in the casino trenches.

And I'm still fighting.

CHAPTER 3

CRAPS

The dice tables of a casino are where you'll often find unfettered excitement. You can hear the cheers from the far reaches of the largest casinos. Some seasoned players, though, would probably say you don't hear it enough. And I would probably concur. The game is known for its streakiness, if there's such a word, streaks of hot and cold that test the mettle of the toughest players trying to outguess the dice. But when those infamous hot streaks do happen, the casino bosses tend to get a little worried. Really. Depending on who's at the table—high rollers or low rollers—a hot run of winning numbers could cost the casino hundreds of thousands of dollars, if not millions.

Some players win a few hundred thousand, others win a few hundred. It's like a dice dealer told me years ago: "Players don't react quickly enough, and they don't bet enough, during a hot streak." It's absolutely true. But I have yet to find anyone who can accurately point out when a table is about to get hot.

The excitement of craps—*noisy* excitement—means players are winning. It beckons more players, and potential players who just watch. They are, for some reason, afraid to jump in. Let's hope that this chapter will clear the air about this game's unfortunate stigma: "It's complicated." I hear it all the time, and when I hear it I know that I'm listening to someone who doesn't play. Because the game isn't the least bit complicated. It's almost as easy as playing slots. Really.

You don't even need to know the odds on your winning bets, but most players want to know so that they can be sure the dealers are paying them correctly. And you don't even need to know most of the bets, because most of the bets, as you'll soon learn, are not the smart bets to make, anyhow. There's only three bets to make, and two of them are virtually identical—just made at different times, that's all—so, we're talking two bets. Do you think that sounds complicated?

Let's learn the game, uncover some secrets, and make some serious money!

HOW TO PLAY THE GAME

Let's first consider the dice. There are two dice in play, with each cube having six sides: 1 through 6. That means that numbers from 2 through 12 can be made when two dice are rolled.

Let's make an important distinction right now. The odds of rolling these 11 numbers vary. The odds of rolling a 4, for example, are much higher (harder) than rolling a 7. There are only three ways you can roll a 4 (2-2, 1-3, and 3-1); there are six ways you can roll a 7 (2-5, 5-2, 1-6, 6-1, 3-4, and 4-3).

THE PASS-LINE BET

Let's list the numbers somewhat out of order so that you can best see what the numbers mean for the most common dice wager, the "pass-line" bet. Here are the numbers in groups for you to remember. Always think of the numbers exactly as I've separated them.

2–3–12	7–11	4–10	5–9	6–8
Craps (loser)	Natural (winner)	Point-Numbers (must be repeated to win)		

It's important to remember the point-numbers in the pairs as I've listed them. You'll find out why later in this chapter.

Each of the numbers 2, 3, and 12 is called a "craps," and it's a loser on the first roll, called the "come-out roll," for all bets on the pass line.

Each of the numbers 7 and 11 is called a "natural," and it's a winner on the come-out roll. The remaining numbers 4, 5, 6, 8, 9, and 10 are called "point numbers," and when one of these numbers is rolled on the come-out roll, that same number must be rolled again before a 7 is rolled in order to win the pass-line bet.

A new come-out roll always follows a pass-line decision, win or lose.

If a 7 rolls on the come-out roll, the pass line wins. If a 3 rolls on the come-out roll, the pass line loses. If a 6 rolls on the come-out roll, there is no win-or-lose decision at that moment. The shooter rolls again, and again, however many times necessary, for either the 6 to repeat (in which case the pass line wins), or for the 7 to roll (in which case the pass line loses).

All other numbers are of no significance to the pass-line bet while the shooter is trying to repeat a point number (called "rolling for the point").

Now you can see why the 7 sometimes wins and sometimes loses. **If the 7 is thrown on the come-out roll, it wins. But if the 7 is made while the shooter is rolling for the point, then the 7 loses.** And that's called a "seven-out."

The dice then pass to the next player, moving in a clockwise direction, and it becomes that player's turn to shoot, starting with a new come-out roll. As long as a shooter does not seven-out, the shooter retains the dice.

Incidentally, if it's your turn to shoot, and you don't want to shoot, that's fine. Simply tell the dealer to "pass the dice," then it becomes the next player's chance to shoot.

When you become more familiar with the game, I'm sure you'll want to shoot. It's fun. All you have to do is toss the dice to the opposite end of the table from where you're standing, and try to bounce both dice off the far wall of the table. It's easier to lightly toss the dice than it is to roll them, especially if you're standing at the far end of a table.

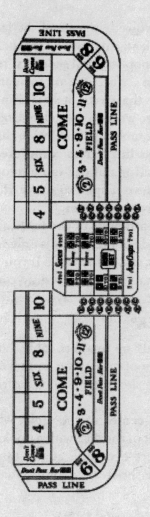

This is a typical Las Vegas layout, although some newer layouts follow the Atlantic City rule of eliminating the "Big 6 and 8" bets on the corners. It's a silly bet that pays 1 to 1 (even money) if a 6 (or 8) is rolled before a 7. The bet should pay 6 to 5. Even a place-bet on 6 or 8 will pay 7 to 6. Players who bet the Big 6 and 8 are showing their inexperience.

Another variation is the field-bet, where some layouts pay double on *both* the 2 and 12. Others pay triple on *either* the 2 or 12, as shown here (triple on 12). Most new casino venues are using the "Las Vegas" layout.

There's no skill involved, in spite of the fact that many dice players have this notion that there are good shooters and not-so-good shooters. It's all a part of the game... just one of so many unique aspects of craps that makes it so exciting.

Now let's pretend to walk up to a table. Look at the illustration of the table layout. **Notice that the area marked "pass line" runs completely around the player sections of the table in order that all players have a spot to make this wager... directly in front of them.**

Also notice that both ends of the table are identical. The right side of the layout is only for players standing at that end of the table. If you're at the left end of the table, you need only concern yourself with that part of the layout.

FOLLOW THE "PUCK"

When you first walk up to a dice table, how do you know if the shooter is about to make a come-out roll or if the shooter is rolling for the point?

The dealer at the center of the table, who controls the movement of the dice with a hooked stick, will usually alert everyone at the table what's going on. If the shooter is about to make a come-out roll, the dealer will announce that the dice are "coming out." If the shooter is rolling for the point, the dealer will make that clear also, by announcing that "the shooter's point is 8," or simply "rolling for 8."

Another way to make this determination is to look at the numbered boxes at the back of the layout and locate the "puck," which has a white side and a black side. The white side says "ON" and the black side says "OFF." The puck is about four inches in diameter and looks like a hockey puck; you'll have no trouble finding it.

Those big boxes at the back of the layout represent the point numbers. At each end of the table there's a box for the 4, 5, 6, 8, 9, and 10. If the shooter is rolling for the point, the puck will be placed within the box of the point number the shooter is rolling for. When the puck is placed in one of these point boxes, the white side (ON) is up. If the puck is in the box marked "SIX," that's the point number the shooter is after.

If the puck is noticed with the black side (OFF) showing, it's usually found in an adjacent box marked "Don't Come" which relates to an entirely different bet, but that's the spot the dealers use to place the puck when the next roll is a come-out roll.

As you might imagine, it's more likely that a shooter will be trying to repeat a point number when you walk up than to be throwing a string of craps or naturals on a come-out roll. So at that instant that you walk up to the table, the shooter will probably be rolling for the point. Possibly, you timed it perfectly and the shooter is about to make a come-out roll.

That's your signal to make a pass-line wager. Incidentally, never make a pass-line bet while the shooter is trying to repeat a point number because then it's a bad bet. I'll tell you why later on.

When the shooter wins, everyone on the pass line wins! Unlike "street" craps, all the players at the dice table are playing against the house, not each other. In gambling jargon, the house is "banking" the bets.

A GAME OF ODDS!

The next bet to learn is called an "odds bet," and it's directly associated with the pass-line bet that you now know how to make. But before we can understand the odds bet, we have to learn what odds means, and what the correct odds are at a dice table for all the possible numbers.

It's important that you know the odds because it tells you how you will be paid when you win. It's your way of checking the payoff to make sure you were paid correctly.

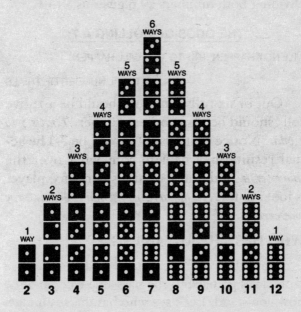

In this Probability Chart, it's readily apparent that there are more ways to roll a 7 than any other number. "Probability" means the same thing as odds: it's easy to compute if you have to.

We know there are 36 ways to roll the dice. And we know there are six ways to roll a 7. That means there must be 30 ways to *not* roll a 7 (36 minus 6). So our odds of rolling the 7 are 30 to 6. Dividing both numbers by 6 gives us 5 to 1.

THE ODDS OF ROLLING A 7:

WILL NOT HAPPEN —⑤ TO ①—WILL HAPPEN
└— + —┘ TOTAL NUMBER OF TRIALS

Out of six rolls, one roll should be a 7; five rolls should be some other number. *That's 5 to 1 odds.* Notice that I said "should be." The actual results may deviate somewhat over the *short term*, and that's what a smart dice player is looking for. *An opportunity when the odds have wavered.*

WHO HAS THE ADVANTAGE?

Now that you understand odds at the dice table, let's go back to the pass-line rules and see how you stand. Let's see who has the advantage.

OK, we know there are four ways to throw a craps and eight ways to make a 7 or 11. Wait a minute! We have an edge here! You bet we do. **The player always has a strong advantage on the come-out roll.**

There must be a catch. And there is. The point numbers! When the shooter has established a point, the casino gets the edge. But not by much. Again, it's easy to see why.

There are six ways to make the 7, and remember that the 7 loses when a shooter is rolling for the point. No point number can be made *six* ways. Your best chance of rolling a point number before a 7 is if the point is 6 or 8, since both of these numbers can be made *five* ways.

Never make a pass-line bet after the shooter has established a point number. That's a dumb move! You're giving up the best part of a pass-line wager—the come-out roll—where you have an edge, and you're getting down just at the time when the casino gets the nod. Not too smart!

The next logical question is who has the edge when you take both the come-out roll and rolling for point numbers into account? Not surprisingly, the casino gets the prize, but it's a cheap one. The casino advantage, overall, is 1.41 percent.

This percentage may seem relatively low, but it's actually a significant concern. There are ways to reduce it and you are about to learn how.

ALWAYS REMEMBER
POINT NUMBERS IN PAIRS

You should now be able to see why we combined the point numbers in our earlier chart... 6 and 8, 5 and 9, and 4 and 10. They were combined because the ways to make them are the same for both numbers in each pair. Accordingly, when odds are given for any point number, it's always the same for its sister point number in the pair.

Remember the point numbers in pairs. That's important.

THE ODDS BET

Now that we really understand odds, we can learn how to make the important odds bet. This wager is made only when the shooter has established a point number. Place your odds bet directly behind the pass-line bet, but not in the pass-line area.

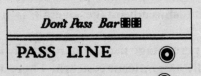

Notice that the odds bet is placed outside of the live area. A triple-odds bet is shown.

The casino will allow you to bet an amount that can be more than your pass-line bet. How much more depends on the casino. Some casinos will allow only two-times odds, called "double odds." Some casinos will let you bet three-times odds, called "triple odds." The more aggressive casinos may go as high as five-times and even ten-times odds. There are casinos in Las Vegas that often banner their craps odds on their marquee, boasting 100-times odds! What's the big deal, you ask?

The odds bet is a fair bet. The casino doesn't earn a penny on this wager. It's paid at the correct odds of rolling a point number before rolling a 7! Your wager on the pass-line is only paid at even money, regardless of the number. But the odds bet is paid at "true odds." *It's the bet that fortunes are made of!*

Here's a chart that gives you the correct odds of repeating point numbers before a 7 rolls. It's important that you remember these odds because they tell you how you will be paid if you win.

POINT NUMBER	CORRECT ODDS OF REPEATING BEFORE A 7
6 & 8	6 to 5
5 & 9	3 to 2
4 & 10	2 to 1

Let's say that the shooter established 4 as the point. If you have $5 bet on the pass-line, you can make an odds bet of $15 at a triple-odds table. If the shooter successfully repeats the 4, you will be paid $5 for the pass-line wager and $30 for the odds bet! Look at the chart. The correct odds of repeating a 4 before rolling a 7 is 2 to 1. That's why your odds bet won $30.

The odds bet is just another example of why the game of craps is so unique. There is no other bet in the casino that does not provide a casino advantage!

Logically, you might ask why make such a big deal about a bet that only "evens out" over a long term. Let me answer your question with my own question. Would you rather make bets that always give the house a rock-solid advantage, or would you prefer a bet that's truly fair? A bet in the casino that doesn't favor the house *is* a big deal!

THE ODDS BET REDUCES THE OVERALL CASINO ADVANTAGE

Making the odds bet along with the pass-line wager reduces the casino's total pass-line advantage from 1.41 percent to about 0.85 percent. Double odds reduces the house edge even more to about 0.63 percent. Triple odds and ten-times odds and so on can reduce the percentage even more, to well under one-half percent!

Although the odds bet does not directly affect the house percentage on the pass-line part of the wager, it does lower the percentage for the total amount of your wager. And in reality, that's what you should be concerned about.

The key to using multiple odds bets is in the way you "size" your bets. Let's compare a pass-line wager of $15 with no odds to another pass-line bet of $5 with $10 in odds. If the point is 10, you would be paid only $15 in winnings for the $15 pass-line wager, compared to $25 for the $5 pass-line bet with $10 in odds. See? It depends on how you structure your bets to earn the advantage of multiple odds without increasing your total risk.

It's worth noting, however, that high multiple odds can be risky. Even triple odds can sting if the dice are not passing (winning). So use common sense in making these bets. **Some players use the odds bet as a betting progression of sorts, starting out with double odds, and then** moving up to triple odds, then four-times odds, and so on, as long as winnings accumulate. If they lose a bet, they go back down to double odds and start over. It's a betting strategy well worth considering. I strongly recommend that you use it.

THE COME BET

The come bet is best described as a "delayed" pass-line wager. And there's no question where to place it. The largest block of the table layout is assigned for come bets. The area has the name "COME" boldly displayed in the center.

You make come bets while a shooter is rolling for a point. That's the only time you can make a come bet since it's basically just like a pass-line bet.

And the same rules apply, which I'm sure you have memorized by now: A 7 or 11 wins on the come, a 2, 3, or 12 loses. Any other number becomes the point number and must be repeated before a 7 rolls in order to win.

Let's say the shooter's point number to win on the pass line has been established as 6. If you wish to have another bet working for you that's just like the pass-line bet, simply place your bet in that section of the come area nearest to your position at the table.

Hope for either an 11 or a point number, because a craps will lose your come bet; a 7 will win your come bet but will lose the pass line.

Let's say the next number rolled is a 9. So now you'll be looking for another 9 (before a 7) to win your come bet. It can be said that you have two numbers working: 6 "on the line" and 9 "coming."

When a 7 or 11 is rolled while your bet is sitting in the come, the dealer immediately places the payoff directly beside your bet. It's your responsibility to immediately pick up the chips, otherwise the bet works on the next roll as another come bet. On the other hand, if a craps is thrown, the dealer simply takes your come bet and it's up to you if you want to make another bet.

If the roll is a 7, the winning come bet is called a "last come," and is often forgotten by players making it, especially if that 7 signaled a time to quit. Dealers often yell to players as they exit the table, "Hey, buddy, you forgot your last come!"

THE POINT BOXES

So now you know that come bets are settled in the come for rolls of 7s or 11s or craps. But if the roll is a point number, your come bet does not remain in the come area. The dealer will reposition your bet in the proper box for the point number rolled and in a spot within that box that's directly referenced to your location at the table. It's the only way that the dealer can keep track of the ownership of bets.

If you're standing along the front of the table, for example, the come bet will be moved to the front of the point box corresponding to your position at the table. If you're standing along the end of the table, your come bet will be moved to the back of the point box. Think of the boxes as having four chip positions along the front for the four potential players along the front of the table, and four chip positions along the back for the four potential players along the end of the table.

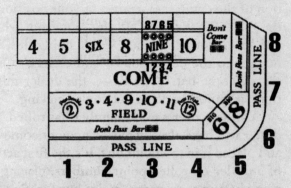

Dealers refer to players at a table by their position, placing come bets and place bets in the corresponding position within the point-boxes. Dealers, in communication with other dealers, also identify players by this position, such as 2-right, or 3 left (right or left of the "stick").

Incidentally it's a good idea to keep an eye on your bets in the point boxes. Don't rely on the dealer to keep all the bets straight.

Since the come bet is just like the pass-line wager, you can take odds on the come bet, too. And you'll definitely want to do that. Here's how:

HOW TO MAKE AN ODDS BET FOR A COME BET

To make the all-important odds bet on a come bet that went to a point box, simply position the bet (you know the routine) in that section of the come area nearest to your position at the table. That's right. In the same spot where you made your come bet. While doing this, announce to the dealer loudly and clearly, "Odds on my come bet." Otherwise, the dealer might think it's another come bet you're making.

You see, after a point number has rolled, the dealer will have already picked up your come bet and placed it in the point box. It's the first action of a dealer on rolled point numbers: placing all come bets in their proper point box location.

When the come bet and odds bet are repositioned in the point box, the dealer places your odds bet on top of the come bet, but offset slightly to distinguish the odds bet from the come bet.

When the shooter repeats a come-bet point for you, the dealer will immediately return your come bet and odds bet to the come area where you originally placed them. Next, the dealer will place your winning chips directly beside the bets. Again, if you don't pick up all the chips, they work on the next roll as another come bet. Be careful!

Let me repeat an important aspect of what you've just learned: When you make a come bet and odds bet, always be sure to position the bets in the come area near the perimeter of the come area and in direct line with where you're standing. Don't just throw your chips down or place them anywhere in the come area. Your bets may later be confused with another come bet placed by another player. It's your responsibility to keep track of your own bets. There's always some jerk at the tables who thinks your chips are his chips.

WHY MAKE COME BETS?

The best reason I can give you for making come bets, *with odds*, is to gang up on the table when a shooter is repeating a lot of point numbers that would otherwise be useless to you if you're just betting the pass line.

Don't let all those beautiful numbers go to waste. That's your cue to make a come bet or two. But, as we talked about in the case of multiple odds, don't go overboard on come bets, either! And, like multiple odds, you can use come bets as a form of betting progression. **Start out by just betting the pass line. If you win a few bets, make a come bet. If you continue winning, make another.**

When a shooter's on a roll, I might have as many as three come bets working for me. When one hits, I start another one so that I always have three bets in the boxes. When the inevitable 7 clears the table, I go back to my basic pass-line-only status and wait for another streak of wins before I begin launching come bets again.

OFF AND ON

Let's say you have a come bet on 6, and decide to fire off another come bet so that you can have two come bets in action. You make the bet, and the shooter throws your 6. If the come bet you just made and the come bet sitting in the point box are of the same value (not counting odds) then the dealer will simply pay your winnings beside the come bet in the come area instead of moving the chips about. Pick up your winnings and let your new come bet stay there awaiting another roll.

If the come bets are not of the same value, it could be confusing to figure out the net winnings. Never let a dealer do this. Insist that the come bet with odds that hit is paid, and the new come bet is moved to the same box awaiting your new odds bet, essentially creating a new bet.

OFF ON THE COME OUT

You can remove your odds bets at any time, or simply call them "off" whenever you like, on a whim or whatever. But there's no particularly good reason for doing it.

Of course, you can't remove a pass-line bet or come bet. Otherwise, you would have a healthy advantage as I told you earlier, by just letting the bets work on the come out roll (where you have a big advantage) and then simply taking the bets down if a point number is established (where the edge swings to the casino). Obviously, the casinos won't go for that!

But since the odds bet is fair, no advantage either way, casinos will let you do as you please with it.

However, **casinos have a standing rule that all odds bets are automatically off on the come-out rolls unless you say otherwise.** The theory is that most players don't want to lose the odds bets in case a 7 is rolled on the come out, which would wipe out all the come bets in the point boxes. The 7, in fact, does wipe out your come bets, but with the odds called off, the dealer will return all your odds bets to you. It's a standard house rule, so go with it.

PLACE BETS

For the players who are too anxious to get their money on the table, especially on their "favorite" point numbers, casinos allow bettors to "place" any or all of the point numbers without having to go through the rigmarole of waiting for them to come up as a come-bettor must do.

But for this luxury, you have to pay a price. Certainly the casino won't pay true odds as it does on your odds bets. No way! Here's a schedule of how the casino pays place bets.

PLACE NUMBER	ODDS PAYOFF	SHOULD BE	CASINO ADVANTAGE
6 & 8	7 to 6	6 to 5	1.52%
5 & 9	7 to 5	3 to 2	4%
4 & 10	9 to 5	2 to 1	6.67%

Placing the 6 or 8 is not a bad bet at all; a meager 1.52 percent house advantage. Occasionally, I'll catch myself placing a 6 or 8 if the number's not covered with a come bet. Still the casino edge is two and one half times greater than a pass-line bet or come bet with double odds. But don't let that stop you if you want to make place bets, because **the 6 or 8 place bets are the most likely place bets to streak.**

In the event you do place a 6 or 8, *be sure to make your wager in multiples of $6, because the payoff is 7 to 6*. For example, if you bet $30 on the 6, the payoff is $35.

Place bets are positioned in the point boxes by the dealers in a similar fashion to come bets. However, you must tell the dealer what the bet is that you want to make. It's not a big deal. You don't have to carry on a conversation. If you want to bet $6 on the point of 8, simply say, "Six-dollar 8."

ONE-ROLL BETS

There are many popular one-roll bets known as "proposition" bets where you either win or lose on the next roll. Perhaps the most popular bet is simply known as "eleven," also affectionately known as "yo." And the most popular time to bet eleven is on the come-out roll. The house advantage on this wager is a little over 11 percent! Which makes it easy to remember, right? Eleven percent for number eleven!

The two other popular one-roll bets are aces and twelve. There's only one way to make either of these bets: You better see one dot on each die for aces, and a trainload of dots on the dice for a 12.

These two bets torment dice players more than any other. Rarely does a player bet them both; it's usually one or the other. And you know what that means, right? If you bet aces, the train pulls in. If you bet the train, two little dots will laugh in your face. The solution, of course, is to bet them both, but you know what will happen, right? You'll see one die with one dot and the other die with six dots. Well, it's a 7. At least you won the pass line.

Betting on any craps is another one-roll bet that's commonly seen; all the craps numbers, 2, 3, and 12 are in play for this 7 to 1 wager. Some players who have worked their pass-line bet up to a significant amount will often make an "any" bet to "insure" their pass-line wagers. But the cost is high: 11 percent.

HARD-TO-RESIST HARDWAYS

Most popular among the proposition bets are hardways, but they are not one-roll bets, which probably explains their prevalence among players. As with the other "prop" bets we've covered, the percentages are steep, but that ominous fact doesn't seem to stop players from loading up on them. Whether they just don't know or just don't care is hard to say. But from a personal perspective, I would conclude that they *do* know and they *don't* care because they are willing to fight the odds for the bigger payoffs.

Players who know me, or who have read other books I've written about craps, know that I've often related stories about huge wins at the dice tables that resulted from an incredible string of hardway hits. With the higher payoffs for these bets, significant wins can come quickly.

When I bet them, however, I treat them as loaded guns; they get all of my respect not only for what they can do when they hit, but for what they can do when they *don't* hit. They'll eat away at your stake like termites on a log cabin! Accordingly, I only bet them after I've already raided the casino's till. That's right. Only when I'm up.

Still, the thrust of this book is to play the percentages, which means, of course, finding the low-percentage games *and* the low-percentage bets. Hardways simply fall short. If you do decide to twirl the cylinders on these bets, remember, *only when you're up!*

As with all the other bets, hardways are simple to make and simple to understand. Here's the gist: The point numbers 4, 6, 8, and 10 are the only ones that can be made in pairs. If a 4 rolls as a pair of 2s, it rolled "the hard way." If it rolled as 3-1, it rolled "easy." But winning the bet isn't easy because you lose it when a hardway rolls easy or a 7 clears the table.

ODDS VERSUS PERCENTAGES

A player-friend of mine called me after he got back from a gambling trip and said he bet twelve hardways during a few hours of play, and hit none! "Boy," he said, "You're right about these high-percentage bets!"

When I told him that the high percentages had nothing to do with it, it left him in a daze. He never did understand the difference between odds and percentages.

The percentages on those hardways could have been ten times as high and still have nothing to do with his shutout. What difference would it have made what the percentages were? He never got paid on any bets, so there was no percentage working against him.

He was simply a victim of the odds, but not to any great extent. He was only going after the hard 6s and 8s, which roll at true odds of 10 to 1. So, in eleven shots, he should have won a hardway, maybe none, maybe two. He took twelve shots; he got none. Big deal.

Remember, anything's possible in the short term, but his "term" was exceptionally short. Besides, he would have needed to take it into the *long* term to see the percentages really work (against him). Over the long term, he would have lost by the difference in true odds and paid odds (10 to 1 vs. 9 to 1). An accumulation of "short pays" would have been his percentage "cost." But those twelve trials were hardly a long-term test.

Now you know: You can't always blame the percentages! Sometimes they're not even in the game! Remember, anything can happen in the short term; you can just about throw the percentages out the window.

My friend could very well have called me up and said he hit three or four of those hardways (out of twelve shots) instead of hitting none, and that wouldn't have surprised me, either. If he said he hit all twelve, I would probably have thought he was hitting the sauce, too.

Incidentally, the odds expression for prop bets in the center of the layout is defined as "for 1" in some casinos, instead of "to 1," such as 10 for 1 in the case of the 6 or 8 hardways, instead of stating 9 to 1 as most casinos do. Both expressions are the same in terms of winnings; the difference is simply whether your bet stays up or is given back to you with your winnings. Odds of 9 to 1 means that you win 9 times your wager and your wager stays up; odds of 10 for 1 means that you are paid 10 times your wager but your wager is taken down.

Stating the odds as 10 for 1 may lead unsuspecting players to believe that they are getting a better payoff. It's a cheap ploy that the casinos should be ashamed of. Both expressions are the same in terms of winnings; the difference is simply whether your bet stays up or is given back to you with your winnings. Odds of 9 to 1 means that you win 9 times your wager and your wager stays up; odds of 10 for 1 means that you are paid 10 times your wager but your wager is taken down.

BET	PAYS	SHOULD PAY	CASINO ADVANTAGE
Hard 6 (or 8)	9 to 1	10 to 1	9.1%
Hard 4 (or 10)	7 to 1	8 to 1	11.1

Look at the payoffs for hardways and note that the 6 and 8 hardways pay the same, as do the 4 and 10 hardways, but the 6 and 8 hardways pay more than the 4 and 10 hardways and even sport a slightly lower percentage.

The reason they pay more is because there are more "easy" ways to make them. More ways, in other words, to lose the bet. (Hardways lose when made easy.) So if there are more ways to lose, then they should pay more, and they do. Six and 8 hardways pay 9 to 1. Four and 10 hardways pay 7 to 1.

It's the opposite of what most rookie players would expect because they know that the 4 and 10 point numbers are harder to make, so they just expect the 4 and 10 hardways to pay more, too. But, as I've just explained, they are misguided in their reasoning.

Hardway bets are placed by the dealer at the center of the table. Simply toss your bet to the dealer and announce it: "Five-dollar hard 6." The bet is placed in a box that, unlike the point-number boxes, represents the whole table, not just one end. So, to find your spot in the box, you first have to mentally divide the box in half. If you're standing beside the dealer just left of center, your spot in the box is the left corner formed by the front edge of the box and that invisible line you drew that divides the box. You'll catch on. Don't worry.

As I said, hardways win when point numbers are made in pairs. If you're on the hard 6, you need a 3-3 to win. Any other 6, and there are four of them (1-5, 5-1, 2-4, and 4-2), will lose the bet. Of course, a 7 will lose the bet, too. And it doesn't have to be a seven-out. In most casinos, "Hardways work unless called off," is a standard cry of the dice dealers. That means you'll lose your hardway bets with a 7 on the come-out roll… unless you call them off.

THE "LADY'S BET"

There are so many variations on the one-roll "field bet" today that I can't give you the specific percentages. Let's say around four to five percent. It's a tempting bet to the uninitiated because there are so many "field" numbers that win. But there are more ways to lose, of course.

Suffice it to say that in the days before women really caught on to craps, all they made were field bets. It became know as the "lady's bet." If a woman asked a craps dealer (all male in those days) for a little assistance, the dealer would show her the big box on the layout marked FIELD.

"Put your bet right here, young lady, and if any of those numbers come up, you win."

That's craps? No, that's not craps. That was just a "brush off."

THE "DON'T" BETS

The sections of the table layout marked DON'T PASS and DON'T COME are for betting *with the casino* and against all the other players, assuming they're not all making "don't" bets, too. Technically, "don't" bettors are not betting "with the casino," but they do win when the casino wins, except in one case: When a 12 is rolled on the come out, the "don't" bettor doesn't win; it's a push (a standoff). The percentages are about as small as the "right" side (betting the dice do pass) and the BAR 12, as the push is called, is worth the 1.40 percent house edge.

The only problem with the "don't" bets is that you want a cold table in order to win. You win when the other players lose. You're siding with the enemy.

I never play the "don't" side because it's too darn boring. No excitement. And there shouldn't be. It could be dangerous.

"Don't" bettors should never yell and scream and wave their arms when a shooter sevens out. Even though they won, other players might have lost thousands! Winning on the "don't" with even a smile of arrogance on your face will get you "looks that could kill!" Be sure a security guard is handy if you plan on touting your win to the other players.

If you're the type who likes to antagonize other people, the "don't" bets were designed just for you.

BEYOND THE BASICS

You positively, absolutely must take the odds on your pass-line and come bets. These "fair" bets, as you've already learned, are the only fair bets in the casino! You cannot ignore them. In fact, you should look for the highest odds that you can find.

We need to be clear on this. You are not looking for these high-odds tables because you're going to start play at that maximum level right out of the chute. No. Too risky. The idea is to start with odds that are within your comfort zone... a reasonable multiple. Your plan should be to use the remaining odds available as a progression to work up.

Here's an example. Let's say you start play, as I do, with three red chips on the pass-line ($15), and you are OK with triple odds, as I am. But the table you found offers 10X odds! Win a few hands and work your way up to 5X odds, then 7X, perhaps, and finally all the way to ten-times odds! Sure, you'll be putting $150 behind your three chips on the line, but you will have won more than enough… much more… to cover the loss, if you lose it. And who's to say you're not going to win it? Think positive going up that ladder.

Our proverbial ladder, incidentally, is higher than you think. Even if you hit the 10X odds on the pass line, you probably have some come bets working for you, too (I would hope so, if a few pass-line wins have been stashed away), so get those come bets moving up the ladder, too!

How you wish to structure your progression is up to you. Just keep the Number One goal in mind: To cash in on a hot streak of numbers for all you've got! That's right! Pull out all the stops! Strike hard! Those nice, long hot streaks don't happen often; you must learn how to recognize the opportunity early on, and start climbing that mountain of cash!

The secret of taking full odds, or at least working your way up there, is not commonly known to beginning players. But you would think that seasoned players know all about it. Well, apparently not.

Recent casino studies have shown that only about ten percent of players take more than double odds when more is offered. That means that 90 percent of all players are *not* taking advantage of a key opportunity.

Go figure.

I can't end this discussion until we talk about the problems of players who visit "regional" gambling markets, perhaps with one or two casinos, and are unable to find 10X odds at the craps tables. They can't find it because there's not enough competition in these smaller venues to produce better game rules for the players. So, let's say you were only able to find 5X odds. You can still make a mini-progression out of it, starting with double odds and working your way up, one increment at a time, to full odds.

Regardless of the playing conditions you find, always take at least double odds when you begin play. If the casino only offers double odds, I suggest you avoid it and look for something better.

By not offering higher multiple odds, these "non-competitive" casinos have taken a valuable option away from you. In my home state of Michigan, we have 24 casinos, mostly Indian casinos, and a bevy of rule variations. When I play in my home state, it's not unusual for me to drive an extra couple of hours to play at a 10X odds table. It's worth it.

Today, I won't play craps in a casino that does not offer at least 5X odds. I suggest you take the same staunch position as I do.

If you play often, well into the long term, it behooves you to play the percentages. The craps table offers a range of bets that runs from as low as 0.3 percent (the pass-line or come with full odds) to as high as 16.67 percent for a prop bet known as "any 7." If you only play the pass-line and make occasional come bets with triple-or-better odds, you *are* playing the percentages. So, what I'm telling you, I guess, is forget all the other bets. It's sage advice. You can't play smarter than making only the lowest percentage bets available.

All of the high-percentage bets are these infamous prop bets found at the center of the table layout and in the "field." From hardways to one-roll bets chasing down aces or trains* (double six), the percentages are at least 9 percent (about half of that for field bets).

Inasmuch as I've promoted hardway bets in several of my other writings,** the smart approach to this game, *especially if it's going to run into the long term*, is to simply play the percentages. And that means pass-line and come bets with full odds. That simple. And you're right. It does simplify the game!

But there's a couple of place bets, placing the 6 or placing the 8, that only cost a player 1.52 percent. Seems reasonable enough, but it's three times the cost of pass-line bets and come bets

---

*The old terms, "snake eyes" for aces and "boxcars" for double six, have become passe; using these terms will generally give you away as a rookie player. Avoid these terms and any of those other slang expressions you might have heard. If you say, "Baby needs a new pair of shoes" (referencing the point of 4), today's players will laugh at you.

**The author's well known "bomb" strategy for beating craps, outlined in his works *How To Win* and *Commando Craps & Blackjack*, is based on hardway betting, but only after significant wins have been realized on pass-line and come bets. The concept is to take a small portion of these winnings and "build a bomb" on either the hard 6 or 8. With the 9 to 1 payoff, hitting the hardway (the author likes to call them "explosions") can produce sizable gains and have been instrumental in his major victories.

with only triple odds. Still, I make exceptions to my rules, and you certainly can too, and 6&8 place bets are a good example. If I'm riding a nice run of point-numbers and have several come bets working, but not on the 6 or 8, I might place these numbers just to have all the bases covered. It's OK. It's not the smartest move over the long term, but in the short term and under the conditions I just described, who can say?

The 6&8 place bets are popular with many players. In fact, there are some players who only play these bets. The payoffs are easy to compute (7 to 6) and they are the "easiest" to roll among the point numbers. In my book, *Casino Gambling*, I provided these players with a strategy for just these bets. It's never been my intention to chastise players for the way they bet. I certainly don't want to take their fun away. In the case of this unique strategy, called 6&8 Power Press, my hope is that it only adds to their fun while providing an important structure to their betting.

Never begin play with relatively large bets, especially multiple bets scattered over the table. Why put yourself in instant jeopardy? Begin with modest bets and increase the size and number of your bets only if wins accumulate.

It's a common-sense approach that helps temper the temptation. Simply put, it's too easy—and too tempting—to make too many bets.

Remember, start small and build!

Playing with a high-roller friend of mine years ago, I got tired of seeing him get knocked out early time and time again. I had a feeling that he was getting tired of it, too! So I told him to play as I do: Start with three red chips on the pass line and see what happens. Well, let me tell you what happened.

Three chips on the line, lost with an ace-deuce. Another three chips, another ace-deuce. Three more chips and then six more behind them as he placed the odds for the point of 4. Three chips in the come, lost with aces.

I stopped him. We watched as a cold dice table finally relented and took him out of his misery with a seven-out. But he wasn't miserable at all. At the coffee shop later, I told him he had just saved about three thousand dollars! "No!" he said. "Closer to four! I feel like I won!"

He did! But he actually won more than that. From that day on, he never again jumped into a game with money flying. To borrow his expression, he would always "test the table with red" before he wrote the big marker.

And if he did write a marker, he would always ask for a couple hundred in green chips instead of all black, two thousand in black, like he used to. The green chips were part of his progression up the color ladder: starting with red, to green, and, hopefully, to black. Stacks of black! With wins stacked behind him!

At the craps tables, always expect the unexpected. Anything can happen in short-term play! Always be prepared to react to a sudden surge in either direction. Good dice players are focused on the game, keyed to the moment. You don't want to miss out on a nice run of numbers, and you don't want to overstay your welcome, either!

Craps is a little different from other casino games in the sense that it tends to run in streaks. Since a 7 ends a hand while a shooter is rolling for a point, I guess we can credit those one in six odds of rolling that 7 for creating the streaky nature of the game. Although the odds are solid in the long term, they're a little shaky in the short term. That 7 might show up prematurely or it might show up late.

To help you remember this important aspect of the game, look at the previous sentence and find the two words that don't belong. You got it! The words *prematurely* and *late* are clearly inappropriate. Just as there is no such thing as an overdue number or color at the roulette wheel, there are no premature or late 7s at the dice tables.

The game is random. You have to expect wild swings in probability, all well within the bounds of mathematical expectation. In other words, when you walk up to a table, learn to expect anything! Anything can happen!

There's no reason to act surprised with a string of quick seven-outs. By the same token, there's little reason to be surprised when the 7 decides to go into hiding. Among all these things that can happen, a nice run of point-numbers would be greatly appreciated. A shooter throwing number after number while rolling for his point is what you're looking for. It's fun when the dealer just keeps giving you chips. Another number; more chips. After all, it's what you're looking for, and I hope you find it often!

Every good dice player knows that you can toss out the odds in the short term because anything can happen. Now you know it, too.

Keep your play in the short term to increase your chances of winning. Allow me a short "secret," if you don't mind. It's so important that I purposely want to keep it short... and sweet, and easy to remember.

I've always believed that the dice tables challenge your disciplines more so than any other casino game. One of my own personal disciplines is playing in sessions, with breaks in between. Short-term sessions are part of my standard casino routine, regardless of the game I'm playing.

Now don't get me wrong. If I'm winning, I'll stay at the table. I'm not going to close up shop while the dice are dancing! I'm not stupid! As long as I'm winning, I play. But if I walk into an instant cold streak, the session will be especially short. And I don't have to see icicles to know that I picked the wrong time.

Even if I'm caught up in that typical win-four, lose-five scenario (seasoned dice players call this "choppy"), I see no reason to keep playing so I take my break.

I'm not there to play; I'm there to win.

If I'm not winning, I'm not playing.

CHAPTER 4

POWER PROGRESSIVE STRATEGY

Over the years, gaming authors have moved away from "systems" that do little to increase your chances of winning. When I started writing about gambling in 1979, one of my first published articles was a thorough whitewashing of the concept of systems. I debunked even the most complex systems, showing readers how and why they would fail.

Not surprisingly, many of the older systems that had at least some "interesting" merit were reprised in the late '90s, many of them "revised" versions, and are still being circulated to this day.

Once again I became intrigued, knowing that we now have a new tool to analyze systems through literally billions of trials.

Using my analytical experiences of the past and the computer power of today, I've refined these "revised systems" to more resemble a "strategy." How? By closely following the mathematical likelihood of winning progressions. The most powerful of these strategies is called the "Power Progressive Strategy," which you will soon learn. It has many advantages that systems never offered.

It will become quite clear to you that strategies have values in many shapes and sizes. For example, it is my belief that a strategy can work even if it sometimes doesn't produce wins as often as you would like; it may, instead, help protect you against losses that you would probably incur otherwise.

If nothing else, a good strategy, like a good plan, gives you an organized, sensible approach to gambling. No more haphazard bets. No more reckless attacks on a game when the conditions say otherwise. There will be reason to your betting... *sound* reason. In fact, even the most tenderfoot of all gamblers will be able to understand the advantages of a strategy over a system.

WHO CAN PROFIT FROM THE POWER PROGRESSIVE STRATEGY?

So, is The Power Progressive Strategy for everyone? Darn near. Or, at least, it should be. The only players we can easily exclude from The Power Progressive Strategy are high rollers. You know, the players think that the only way they can win big is to bet big, right out of the chute! This dangerous notion is entirely hogwash. **You *can* win big without betting big! That's one of the key principles of** The Power Progressive Strategy*!*

The only assurance I can give players who start out with big bets is this: Big losses! Maybe not *every* time but *some* time. And for players like you and me, why take that risk? Indeed. The players who *will* take that risk have money trees growing in their backyard. But having big money is certainly no reason to bet big money. If you are so fortunate to have a lot of money, and you intend to get your thrills and spills by risking it, you're barking up the wrong tree! You're reading the wrong book!

USE THE PPS FOR
EVEN-MONEY WAGERS

The Power Progressive Strategy is designed for even-money wagers, such as blackjack, the pass-line and come bets at the dice tables, and even roulette, for that matter. Although roulette does not sport low enough percentages to be included in this book, it's worth the mention because I know that roulette players will be reading this chapter, and hoping they've found a way to reduce the percentages. Of course, no player can really reduce percentages,* but some players can reduce the odds against them through judicious betting and structured sessions of attack. The best assault on a roulette wheel is a "hit and run" approach.

There is some question as to whether or not the PPS can be used at the blackjack tables while card-counting. Most often, it's used by players who are *not* counting the cards. In my own case, I always incorporate both card-counting and the PPS when I'm at the blackjack tables. If the count is running in my favor, and I'm on a string

---

*Unless they've found a single zero wheel with either enprison or surrender offered. And, I might add, with modest betting limits.

of wins, I'll push the envelope to the max. After all, I've found not one but both of the game attributes I'm looking for: A positive count of remaining cards, and a streak of winning hands. Can it get any better?

THE MANY BENEFITS OF THE POWER PROGRESSIVE STRATEGY

As a result of my many years studying the games and, particularly, the players, it became clear to me what most players really want from gambling. Obviously, players want to win, but it's *how* they win that determined the four important traits of The Power Progressive Strategy that make it unique. First and foremost, players want those wins with low risk and high rewards. As any good stockbroker would attest to, it's first on the list of most all new investors. And it's exactly what "investors" in the casino want also: token investments; big returns.

Most all players—even if they don't want to admit it—not only want to win big with little risk, but they also want to win both easily and quickly. It's a sign of the times, I suppose. And it's a tall order. It's why there are fewer players at the racetrack today and more players in casinos. The decisions are faster in the casino—some would say, too fast—and the work factor associated with handicapping is nearly non-existent in the casino.

My analysis also explains why most patrons in casinos today are slot players. Slots definitely offer low risk and high rewards. Just ask the player who won five thousand dollars playing a nickel slot! And slot machines are certainly fast. As fast as you can load 'em up, push the buttons or pull the handle. With the exception of certain skill machines such as video poker, there is absolutely nothing to learn, nothing to study, nothing to memorize. Who would argue that slots are easy to play?

All of this also explains why blackjack has become somewhat flat over recent years. New players coming up soon realize that they must really bone up on the game to have any chance at winning. Only a few make that decision to "work" at the game, to really learn it, much as a chess player must do to really appreciate the complexity and strategy of the game.

Too many players also pass up the craps tables for much the same reason. The table layout looks complicated, even though the game is gosh-awful easy to play.

Gambler's also shy away from horse racing because they find the action far too... well, slow. Except for those "most exciting two minutes in sports," the rest of the time it's b-o-r-i-n-g, because most new players today have no interest in cracking the Racing Form, or studying the program. So they wait, and they wait, for the next race. The new wave of handicappers at a racetrack are not patient. And, as you might expect, they are not winners, either.

So now we have the components of the Power Progressive Strategy that the younger set find attractive. It's low-risk, high reward; it's quick and easy; and it's fast and furious. Oh, that's ony three. There's four. I forgot, it's fun, too. Playing the PPS has to be fun, otherwise, the new wave of players today would shun it. And don't tell me that fun is automatic with playing. Playing isn't fun. *Winning* is fun!

Remember this: **Gambling isn't fun if you are not in control of your play. The Power Progressive Strategy helps keep you in control.**

OK, so The Power Progressive Strategy is low risk, we have a good chance for a decent win, the pace will keep you on your toes, and the experience is, hopefully, fun. Who could ask for more? Well, I could. And I will.

Whenever I play, I must have one driving force always on full power. You might think that you know what it is, but I'll lay odds that you don't. It goes beyond that trite expression: a desire to win. Everyone wants to win. That's no big deal.

You see, I've found that a desire, alone, is not going to get the adrenalin pumping; it's not going to keep me on my toes as I continue to play hard in a manner that I call "controlled aggression." (Simply defined as aggressive but not stupid.)

What works for me is not a reconfirmation of my desire to win; it's so much more than that. Indeed, my "driving force" is what I call "an anticipation of winning big." *That* is the force that energizes me on every deal, every roll, every spin, every game, every race. **I want to know that I might be only one play away from the biggest score of my lifetime!**

But I can't give the casino an on-going battle. No one can. You need to enjoy that anticipation while, at the same time, protecting your arsenal of weapons. I call it "Staying Power," one of my favorite expressions. I create my own staying power, increasing my chances of that big score, through judicious play. For those of you who know me, you know exactly what that means. I'm often on the move. I'm not in a hurry... *never* in a hurry... I'm just moving. A friend of mine says I'm "drawn to the heat." Yeah, I wish. But one thing's for sure; I am an *active* player.

I like to play in short sessions and take breaks in between. It's a hit-and-run approach to gambling that I particularly like. If the table is good, I'll stay until it turns. If the table is *not* good, that session will be extra short.

I'm often asked why I play this way. "What's the difference," someone will ask me, "if you make your next bet a minute later or 20 minutes later?

It's a BIG difference! You see, I want to change the time... the window, the rhythm, the frame, the period, the moment, whatever you want to call it.

I'm a big believer in timing... we all either time it right or time it wrong. Like you, I'm looking for the right time... I'm literally searching for opportunities.

Remember what I said. **Winning is not my motivation. Winning is my objective. My motivation is the *anticipation* of winning. And to that end, I want as many shots as I can take! It's like an old-timer told me many years ago: "You gotta learn how to save your bullets."**

For those of you who don't mind betting some of your winnings right back at the casino, the Power Progressive Strategy requires only modest bets at the outset, but calls for some bigger bets as you progress up a winning streak. It is a simple, yet effective, strategy of reinvesting a portion of your winnings.

Please understand that you must be comfortable with your betting. If, at any time, you're not comfortable with what you're doing, don't do it. Gambling, with all of its inherent stress, can become insurmountable if you are the least bit uncomfortable with your play. You must have confidence in what you're doing, tempered with patience and caution.

These three important betting disciplines: confidence, patience, and caution, are the hallmark of successful players.

THE POWER PROGRESSIVE STRATEGY

This special strategy can be used for all three of the major table-games: craps, blackjack, and roulette.* Because of its frequent use, I believe it would be more helpful to you if we detail the strategy right here, now that we've concluded the chapters on craps and blackjack. Once you learn the basics of this strategy, the concepts of betting will be a breeze for you.

Now that we're ready to talk about the strategy in detail, it's important that you understand another basic set of tenets on which my strategy is based:

The Power Progressive Strategy is based on the concept that in any negative-expectation game, the keys to success are in (1) minimizing the number of decisions, (2) maximizing the wins in winning decisions, and (3) minimizing the losses in losing decisions.

*Although roulette is not a game covered in this book because of its relatively high percetages, I recognize that there are thousands of players using a plethora of strategies, so why not offer the most effective one? Remember, though, the PPS is designed for even-money wagers, so roulette players should only use this strategy for bets such as red/black, odd/even, etc.

By letting patience and frequent exits play a big role in our betting strategies—not to mention the very nature of the bets we will be making, such as avoiding the one-roll bets at craps—we have already taken a good turn at key No. 1. All that's left to do is unleash our winning potential, while holding losses to a minimum.

The Power Progressive Strategy

	$5	
	5	PRE-PLAY
	5	
	10	
	15	RED LEVEL
	20	
Repeat Option	**25**	
	50	GREEN LEVEL
	75	
Repeat Option	**100**	
	200	BLACK LEVEL
	300	
Repeat Option	**400**	
	800	
	1200	PURPLE LEVEL
	1600	
	2000	

The Power Progressive Strategy combines the advantages of optimum betting (making only the lowest percentage bets) with a mathematically proven, quasi-exponential betting progression. It *will* help you maximize winnings and minimize losses.

It even has built-in rules to help minimize exposure. Whether it keeps you out of the long term, however, is up to you. Only you can decide exactly how attached you want to become to your friendly, neighborhood casino.

As I present The Power Progressive Strategy to you, I'm reminded of what we talked about earlier… that too many players today want "easy" and they want "quick." I can make the strategies easy, and, to some extent, quick, but I want you to know right now that "quick" can be a detriment to winning. Players who want to win quickly are the same people who tend to bet recklessly.

I'm not going to compromise my strategies just because some players are so wound up with gambling that they need rapid-fire decisions. I want you to learn how to replace your desire for speed with an enjoyment of "anticipation."

Of all the places where patience is a virtue, none is a better example than the casino. I honestly don't believe players can win with even a modicum of consistency if they do not display patience.

POWER PROGRESSIVE STRATEGY ADVANTAGES

- Makes your betting virtually automatic. There are no tough decisions to make. Nothing to ponder. You simply let the strategy do the work!

- Gives you "out of the gate" protection against sudden losses.

- Ensures a big payday during a hot streak.

- Forces you to bet down or quit during a cold streak.

- Works at all table games.

THE POWER PROGRESSIVE STRATEGY OVERVIEW

Before we go over the important rules for this strategy, let's talk a little about how the strategy works. You might think the design looks rather basic, but there's more to it than meets the eye.

Note that there are five levels to the progression, beginning with pre-play. **Pre-play is your safe harbor. You are not allowed to leave pre-play and enter the progression until you have won three bets in a row.** As a further protection, you must quit the session in pre-play if your starting stake of $40 is ever reduced to $20. You will always leave the table with no less than $20.

Once you enter the progression, continue to increase your bet to the next amount listed as you continue to win. **If you lose at any time during the run, your next bet, called a "drop-down" bet, will always be three betting amounts lower. If you lose that bet, too, it's time to exit the session.**

Remember it this way: **It takes three wins to get in, two losses to get out.**

Chip Color Matches Betting Level

LEVEL	CHIP VALUE
Pre-play/Red	Red $5 Chips
Green	Green $25 Chips
Black	Black $100 Chips
Purple	Purple $500 Chips

Each level will be easy to identify as you play, because your bets will be in the chip color of the levels.

In the first level, you'll play with red ($5) chips, just as you will in pre-play. But in the green level, you'll progress to green ($25) chips. In the black level (everyone's favorite), you'll be betting black ($100) chips... and holding onto your seat. Because the next level, if you get to it, is where the mega-money is: The purple level means you'll be betting purple ($500) chips. Technically, the second bet of this level goes to purple, but it's close enough. (Some casinos use a different color for their $500 chips, but who cares what color they are as long as there are two nice round zeros after the 5.)

Incidentally, if you need to change color as you proceed up the progression, by all means do this. Simply ask the dealer to change your stack of 20 red chips to four green chips, for example. Some dealers tend to pay off bets in the same color, but you want to get "new" color in your payoffs so you can have the right color to start the next level. **It's important that you use the chip colors correctly as you go up the progression. Using the right chip colors minimizes the number of chips in a bet, makes**

payoffs easier, and helps you to know exactly where you are in the progression.

The Power Progressive Strategy's Transition Bets

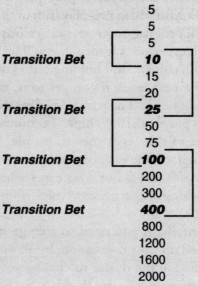

	5
	5
	5
Transition Bet	**10**
	15
	20
Transition Bet	**25**
	50
	75
Transition Bet	**100**
	200
	300
Transition Bet	**400**
	800
	1200
	1600
	2000

An interesting design element of this new progression can be noted with each "transition" bet, the first bet of a new level. Note that this wager is only one unit higher than the previous level, and, in a sense, follows the previous level's progression. This transition bet was carefully designed into the strategy to help ease you along to the next level while extending the diminishing percentage of increase within a four-bet run (10, 15, 20, 25, for example).

THE POWER PROGRESSIVE STRATEGY RULES

IMPORTANT: The progression, per se, is only a part of the strategy, which will not work for you if the strategy rules are not adhered to. *Following the rules is just as important as following the progression.*

1. Take to the session a stake of $40.

2. Enter the session with a pre-play bet of $5.

3. Exit the session if (a) you lose two bets in a row, or (b) your stake drops to $20.*

4. Enter the progression only after you win three bets in a row.

*If you are making multiple craps bets, a loss on one bet, followed by a loss on another bet, is not two losses in a row. Rule 3a applies to each wager. These losses, however, are subject to rule 3b (aggregate wagers). Rule 3a seems too stringent to some readers, but the reasons behind this rule are solid: more breaks, less exposure to negative trends. At blackjack, a split or double down is considered one play. There are no "double" wins or losses. If you split and win one hand and lose the other, it is a "no play."

5. Increase your bet to the next betting amount shown in the progression as long as you continue to win each bet.

6. Decrease your bet by three betting amounts following a loss in the progression. This bet is called a "drop-down" bet.

7. If the drop-down bet wins, continue the progression from that point. If the drop-down bet loses, you must exit the session subject to rule 3a.

8. If you make multiple bets, each bet is treated independently.

EXPLANATION OF THE RULES

Rule 1: Learn how to start each session with the same-size stake. All good gamblers I know do this. It's a mark of discipline. Don't walk up to a table and fish around in your pockets for whatever you can scrounge up. Do you think this looks pro? Have two twenties ($40) ready to go. Exchange them for chips by setting the bills on the table directly in front of you (but not within a betting area) while saying, loud and clear: "Change forty dollars, all red chips, please."

Personally, when I do this at a dice table where the whole table is a betting area, I purposely lay the bills across part of the "field" and part of the "come," two adjacent betting areas within easy reach of the dealer. That way, in case I'm confronted with a deaf dealer, there's no question that my money *doesn't* play.

Ultra-conservative players might be concerned about starting out with $40. They shouldn't be. Forty dollars is *not* a loss-limit. On the contrary. Rule 3b limits your loss for the session to $20.

So, why not start out with $20 instead of $40? Because I also want you to learn how to leave a cold table with a goodly portion of your stake. It may only be psychological, since either way it's a $20 smack in the teeth, but I never want to put you in a position where you walk away with nothing. There's no worse feeling.

Incidentally, just because Rule 3a says you walk at $20, that doesn't mean you can't walk earlier. That's something else I don't want to do; I never want to come across as forcing you to play to a certain limit, or for a certain length of time. *Quit whenever you want to.*

The next thing you do after exiting a session is to go to the cage and exchange the remaining chips for cash. And, if you're like me, you'll record the session in your journal. Doing these things has a secondary purpose: It gives you something to do during your break from the tables. You might even want to get a cup of coffee and plan your next session. Whatever you decide to do, *let patience guide you*. I don't want to see you in a rush to get back to the tables.

This is an important discipline to follow, so allow me to repeat it: Always cash in your chips when you exit a session. Never begin a session with chips. Always begin a session the same way each time: with cash—two twenties.

If you have won a considerable amount of money from prior sessions, lock up your money, literally. Most casinos offer safety deposit boxes at no charge to you. **Never carry large amounts of cash on your person.**

Another advantage of using a safety deposit box is to keep you away from your winnings. I hate to see players risking more than just a small portion of their winnings for stake money.

Key question: So when do you go back and tackle the table again? Is five minutes too soon? You're darn right it is! Take a break. Relax. Eat lunch. Go for a walk. Check out some other tables. Check out the pool. Check out the action. At the tables, that is. What's the point of quitting a bad table if you're going to head right back?

Rule 2: Pre-play starts with $5. And you'll stay at that betting level until you can string three wins together. Since this strategy will be used only for bets with even-money payoffs, which usually have "decent" percentages, you'll encounter that typical win-one, lose-one scenario often. There is little movement in terms of wins or losses, so the $5 betting limit is not going to be much of an issue. No one would say, "Gee, I wish I were betting $25 instead." Breaking even is breaking even.

If you find yourself winning only one bet out of three—and not that unusual, either—you will be thankful that you are restricted to your $5 limit. If, on the other hand, the table conditions look promising, and you've managed to win three out of three, what better indicator to start moving up a little?

When I mention pre-play to some of my friends who bet much more heavily than I do, I get quite a laugh. "Five bucks? You've got to be kidding!" Funny, isn't it? You don't even have to be a high roller to look down your nose at a five-dollar bill. For the high rollers of the world, $5 isn't even good enough for tip money. And it certainly won't get them any comps, either. Too bad. **This book is for players who want to win money, not comps. It's for players who bet to win, not to impress.**

Let's get serious for a moment. Remember that this rule is for openers. What I call "early betting." Judging the potential of the strategy by the $5 pre-play bet is like watching a quarterback on the opening drive, and then deciding whether or not he's going to carry his team to victory. There's so much of the game left to play! It's how the game ends up, hours later, that counts. Sure, you might have seen him fumble on that opening drive, but now he's piling up the points!

And it's the same thing at the tables. You might start out slowly, but later on you might creep up the progression and run into some decent-sized bets. You might even reach the high rollers' level. Trouble is, with these guys, most of them like to *start* with the big bets. And guess what usually happens.

If players were to see me playing at the beginning of a session, they might be surprised—if not bored—watching me bet a thin nickel at the dice table with an even thinner dime for odds. Five dollars on the pass-line and ten bucks in odds is not going to pop many eyes. No jaws are going to drop.

But I'm not bored. And I really don't care what anyone else thinks about the way I play. I know what I'm doing. I'm busy. I'm hunting. Like most players, I'm after the hot shoot that can send me up the progression. Unlike most players, however, I bide my time in getting there, if I get there. Either way, I enjoy the hunt.

Now if those same players were to see me again at that same table a half-hour or so later, it's possible I might be throwing black chips around like candy. I might have a couple of thousand in chips spread over the table with piles more in front of me! Those players might actually confuse me with a high roller. What an insult! But that's what the Power Progressive Strategy can do for you!

Rule 3: This important rule protects you against the possibility of getting beaten by a negative streak. By limiting the streak to two, we've nipped it in the bud. We're looking for hot streaks, not cold streaks, so it's time to search elsewhere. Why take the chance that these cold streaks will only continue?

Understand that the lose-two-in-a-row-and-you're-out rule applies at any time… in pre-play, or while riding the progression, as Rule 7 also makes clear.

Always keep an eye on your stake. Don't ignore the importance of rule 3b. If your stake ever drops to $20, it's quitting time. It might mean a short session, but who cares. You escaped. You've salvaged half your stake to start a new one. There's always a new session to look forward to. Isn't that right?

Don't think of rule 3b as too strict. It isn't. The critical exit rule is simply to guard against an indiscernible trend. Dice players call this condition "choppy." What it really means is the game is beating you so slowly that you don't realize it. Stop the trend at $20.

Incidentally, don't be concerned that you're exiting sessions too frequently as you apply rule 3. You will definitely find that there are more times than you imagined when the rules tell you to quit. And what you'll be doing is something you probably never did as often as you should have: restricting your losses! But that's not all.

As you can appreciate, the best time to restrict your exposure is when you're losing.

Restrict your losses. Restrict your exposure. Two for the price of one.

Rules 4 & 5: This is the fun part! You won your three nickel bets, you've paid your dues, now you're ready to get strapped in and ride the progression! You'll want to take it as far as it will let you.

As long as you win, proceed to the next betting amount. Just let it happen. Don't be nervous. You'll have plenty of protection from previous wins. There are only three places in the progression where a loss might be… well, let's say… less opportune than others. And those spots are where the bets press, as marked with a notation on the chart that says, "Repeat Option." It means exactly what you think. You have the option of repeating the bet before the press. The theory is that winning the repeat option makes you better-prepared to lose the press. Personally, I don't make repeat options anymore. But you can. It's entirely up to you.

Incidentally, readers write to me on occasion to tell me how high up the progression they've gone. As you can appreciate, most of the time the progression takes you only into the red level. The thinking for most new players is that making it to the green level is just average. No! Getting to the green level is good! *Darn* good!

Getting to the purple level is a great goal to shoot for, but we must be realistic. Reaching the purple level is on a par with hitting 8 out of 8 on a keno ticket. Well, that's not quite true, but the point should be clear. The purple level is an incredible feat!

Rule 6: Yes. All good things do come to an end, sometime. This rule protects you from doing something stupid like continuing the progression after a loss.

There's an old gambler's maxim that certainly applies here: **Never press a loss.** The term *press* means to double the amount of your previous wager in the hope of both winning the bet and making up for the loss.

Indeed, the right move is to *reduce* your bet with a drop-down wager, and that's what Rule 6 tells you to do: Your next bet following a loss in the progression is reduced in proportion to the size of your losing wager. Simply "drop down" three betting amounts and that's your new starting point. Of course, if you were in the red level, your drop-down bet will be in pre-play. And that means you need to follow pre-play rules and win three out of three before you can get out again.

Some players elect to exit the session after a losing bet that ended a lengthy progression. Let's say they were at $100 when they lost the bet. They can't bring themselves to cut back, especially all the way down to a "lowly" $25, so they quit. They had the thrill of betting black, not to mention the thrill of a nice win streak, and they figure they'll be able to appreciate the value of that $25 chip after taking a break, and then starting up again with a nickel on the line. And they are oh-so right. Values diminish as you go back down. After all, you've been there. But going up, you're heading where you probably *haven't* been, which means those betting levels are a new, tasty experience.

So, after a loss, you certainly can quit if you like. Quitting is far superior to continuing the progression, but the smarter choice is to follow Rule 6 and simply cut back by three betting amounts. With all the success you've just had, it's possible the loss was just a blip in your immediate future, and you might be headed right back up again.

Rule 7: This interesting rule covers both situations following a drop-down bet.

If you lose the drop-down wager, that means you lost two bets in a row and you just heard the factory whistle. It's quitting time. No options. No whining. You walk. You exit the session. Your first losing bet, incidentally, was your biggest bet. Your second losing bet was probably big, too, relatively speaking. It would be pure stupidity to risk losing another one.

If you win the drop-down bet while in the progression, continue with the progression at the next amount directly higher than the drop-down bet. For example, if your first loss was $100, your drop-down bet will be $25. If you win that bet, your next wager will be $50. If you lose the $50 bet, your drop-down wager will be $15.

Losses take you down; wins take you up. That's the gist of the Power Progressive Strategy. Doesn't it make sense? It should. It should make all the sense in the world to you.

There's something else you should know before we go on to the last rule. We talked about it while discussing Rule 6; we'll talk about it again. There's nothing that says you can't quit instead of returning to pre-play or making a drop-down bet. If you want to quit, quit! In fact, quit any time you want to, although I can't understand why anyone would want to quit while riding a nice win streak. Most often, if players elect to quit on their own (not being forced to quit by rule), it's usually at that moment when they otherwise would have been relegated to pre-play.

But if you do feel like playing some more, follow the pre-play rules and see if you can re-enter the progression. If pre-play doesn't work out and you're forced to exit the session, go outside and get some fresh air. It's probably time for a break, anyhow.

Rule 8: If you decide to make multiple bets, common at the roulette and dice tables, you must learn how to keep track of these bets as they relate to all the rules, because each bet is a separate bet, independent of each other, and subject to all the rules we've just gone over. However *all* bets are considered combined for the important rule 3b.

It's not unlikely that you might have one bet riding a progression, while another bet or two are resting in pre-play. When you're in the progression, it's easy to tell where you are by simply looking at the size of your wager. *But in pre-play, you need to remember where you stand with the three-out-of-three rule.* Keeping track of one bet is easy. Keeping track of two bets is easy, too. But three bets might take a little doing. Some players I know use a scratch pad. Others keep track by stacking chips in front of them. However you do it, don't release a bet into the progression until it has earned its way.

MINIMUM BETTING

The Power Progressive Strategy, is based on a table-minimum wager of $5. But what if you can't find a $5 table? What if you're reading this book many years after I penned it, and the effects of inflation have taken their toll? We all know about inflation, right? In the casino, it means the table minimums go up but the valet who parks your car still gets the same dollar tip.

But even if you're reading this book in its first printing, you still might have trouble finding a $5 table, especially on holidays and weekends. On Friday night the tables are all $10 minimum. On Monday, and all the other weekdays, those same tables are $5. Well, it's too easy for me to say, "Don't play on holidays or weekends." Some players have no other choice.

You might also have trouble finding a low table-minimum if you play in a market where there is little or no gaming competition. Some one- or two-casino markets have high table-minimums *every* day! And you thought only players were greedy? Guess again.

I have answers to a lot of your gambling problems but I have no answer for this one. **I deplore the concept of setting high table-minimums. I deplore any tactic where the casino is plainly taking advantage of its huge supply of customers. What's worse, I know that most of you will fall for the casino's ploy... because you want to play.**

These higher table-minimums will have a chilling effect on the way you play. Right off the bat you're being pushed, you're being forced into doing something you don't want to do, and you'll find yourself in a foul mood because of it. I can't think of a worse way to begin gambling.

I urge you to look for casinos with reasonable table-minimums, which, outside of Nevada, probably means trying your darndest to play on a weekday.

It is possible to alter the Power Progressive Strategy, but it's a compromise I don't like. An example would be to start pre-play at $10 (assuming a $10-minimum table) and simply start the red level at $15.

A key concept of The Power Progressive Strategy, as you know, is to restrict your initial bets to minimum levels until you start winning. If these initial bets are substantial due to high table-minimums, the casino has just defeated your strategy. As I said, don't give them the opportunity.

CHAPTER 5

VIDEO POKER

If you are one of the multitude of casino players searching for a low-percentage game, but a bit apprehensive about table games, here's your answer: Video Poker!

I was fortunate to have known several of the original inventors and designers of the game, a somewhat radical departure from the traditional slot machine. They were confident they had a winner while the new machine was still on the drawing board.

Video poker, you see, introduced an element of skill to playing a slot machine! Players had choices to make—intelligent choices, hopefully—to improve their winning chances! No zombie-like actions of just pulling a handle, crossing your fingers or closing your eyes, and hoping for a jangle of electronic sounds—bells and buzzers mostly—to indicate a win! Maybe not a big win, but something… something to cause coins to drop into your tray and produce that lovely clinking sound that gives you a chance to show off to your neighbor players. "Hey, Helen, I just hit bars again. Did you hear it? I haven't heard anything coming from your machine. What's the matter, honey, no luck today?"

That frequent sound of coins dropping into a machine's tray is a sound of the past today, except for those rare moments when you push the "cash out" button, but even then there is little clinking. Most astute players place a coin bucket under the machine's ejector to capture all the coins as they spit out. But whether electronic sounds or honest-to-goodness coin-clinking, there just wasn't anything a player could do in those days to make a little more noise.

The guys who put video poker on the market so many years ago were very familiar with the scenario I just related. They suspected that slot players were getting tired of a reliance on luck to beat slot machines, so they concocted video poker as an answer. The Gaming Control Board gave them a "go for launch" in 1976 when hundreds of machines hit the Nevada markets.

There was only one problem. No clinking. Not from these rogue machines, anyhow, machines that apparently looked too complicated to play. But more than that, they didn't look like a slot machine at all!

Slot players, especially in those days, were a fickle bunch; they actually liked the idea that luck was the determining factor—the *only* factor—in whether they won or lost. They didn't *want to do* any thinking, heaven forbid! And they scoffed at the notion that relying on luck was, in some way, only a slot player's misfortune.

"You think luck doesn't play a role at the table games? Luck is part of all the games!" That was one of the many responses from surveys carried out after the video poker machines laid the biggest bomb in slot history. The video poker design team did its job. The marketing and research team apparently didn't.

It would be nearly ten years later when video poker would finally catch on. The slot industry experts today believe it took that long simply to change players' attitudes about winning and losing. Particularly the attitudes of "senior" players, as the industry calls the over-50 gang.

But what really brought the game into widespread acceptance was younger players. They were more technology savvy and more apt to investigate an intriguing new offering. They liked the idea that an element of skill was incorporated into the design.

Sadly, though, many players never did use the skill advantage. They did not develop a skill to lower the percentages. Even today, I see players who have no earthly clue what cards to hold and what cards to toss.

Before we get into the winning secrets of this great game, let's go over the rules and learn the basics. If you're an occasional player, a brief refresher course won't hurt you.

HOW TO PLAY THE GAME

Video poker is basically five-card draw poker. And it's played in much the same way as the live game is played except that you are paid solely for the value of your hand; you do not have to bet it against other players... bluffing and raising and calling and folding and all of that sort of thing. There are no other players to try and outfox to make a weak hand beat a stronger hand, as you might do at the games in the casinos' poker rooms.

Video poker is you against a machine. That's all. And that's the reason many players like it. No intimidation. No pressure. No psychological skills to learn. After all, how could you out-psych a machine?!

Just as a dealer at the live game delivers five cards to each player, the machine game begins the same way: The machine delivers five cards to you on your screen after you have hit the "deal/draw" button.

Now you have a decision to make. You can keep as many cards as you like in order to make the best poker hand. You can keep one, two, three, four, or all five… or you can decide not to keep any. You indicate the cards you want to hold by pushing the "hold" button below each card on the screen.*

---

*Make sure the machine registered your hold of a particular card by displaying the word *hold* on the screen above the card you held. Too often, a poorly maintained machine will not register a card you held, even though you pushed the button. If that happens, and you then push the deal/draw button, the machine will replace the card you thought you held. Machine errors such as this are usually caught by careful players; those who play too fast often miss the malfunction. All casinos have a standard rule that such machine malfunctions are up to the players to catch. You should also report the problem to a floor supervisor.

Now it's time to see if you can improve your hand. Push the deal/draw button again and the machine will remove the cards you didn't hold and replace them with new cards. At this point, the machine will let you know if you have made a winning hand by highlighting on the screen the winning hand you made and paying you for it based on the paytable displayed on the screen.

If you made three-of-a-kind (three cards all of the same value, such as three kings), you'll be paid three times the amount of your wager. *It's important to note, however, that the paytables tell you how much you will "collect," not win, because your bet is not returned.* In our example, you really only won two times your bet since you have to subtract your bet from your winnings. Your net win for three-of-a-kind, therefore, is two times your wager. You were paid 2 to 1.

Since the whole idea is to make the best poker hands, it's obviously essential that you know the rank of hands. Here's a chart to help you. After a few hours of play, the rank of hands will become second nature to you.

RANK OF POKER HANDS
(in descending order)

HAND	DESCRIPTION
Royal Flush	Only the 10, jack, queen, king, and ace of the same suit.
Straight Flush	Any five cards in consecutive value, of the same suit, such as 2, 3, 4, 5, and 6 of diamonds.
Four-of-a-Kind	Any four cards of the same value (all four cards of the four different suits) such as the 8 of hearts, diamonds, spades, and clubs.
Full House	Five cards that include a pair and three-of-a-kind, such as a pair of kings and three 10s.
Flush	Any five cards of the same suit, such as 8, 10, jack, king, and ace of hearts.
Straight	Any five cards in consecutive value, not of the same suit, such as 4 of clubs, 5 of hearts, 6 and 7 of spades, and 8 of diamonds.
Three-of-a-Kind	Any three cards of the same value such as three queens.
Two Pair	Two pairs of equal-value cards such as two 3s and two 10s.
Jacks-or-Better	Any pair of jacks, queens, kings, or aces.

BEYOND THE BASICS

Video poker is the only slot-machine game where you can shop for the best percentages. Why? Because the paytables are not all alike! There are well over a hundred different paytables, although only a dozen or so are frequently found in today's casinos. Clearly, it's important that you learn to recognize and compare the different paytables.

Most often, the determining factor in whether or not a machine is indeed low-percentage is the payout for a flush, full house, and two pair. Based on a one-coin payout, the machine to look for pays six coins for a flush and nine coins for a full house. Two coins are paid for two pair.

Look For This Optimum Paytable:

ROYAL FLUSH	250
STRAIGHT FLUSH	50
4 OF A KIND	25
FULL HOUSE	**9**
FLUSH	**6**
STRAIGHT	4
3 OF A KIND	3
TWO PAIR	2
JACKS OR BETTER	1

On all payouts except the royal flush, the payouts for multiple coins are linear; that is, if the one-coin payout is 6, the five-coin payout is 30. So, if you're looking at a 6-9 paytable showing the payouts for five coins inserted, the payouts for a flush and full house will be 30 and 45 coins respectively.

It's worth noting that the machines you're most likely to find today, including major gaming markets, are called 5-8 machines (five coins for a flush and eight coins for a full house). The percentage on these games, when played with optimum skill, is about 3 percent. In noncompetitive markets, it's not unusual to find 5-6 machines (five coins for a flush, but only six coins for a full house). The percentage is a little over 5 percent... you might as well settle in at a roulette wheel and take your lumps. Clearly, you must avoid the 5-6 and 5-8 machines, playing only machines with 6-9 paytables. I hope you find them.*

*Normally, I would not have to tell you this, but I'm seeing machines today that do *not* return your bet (a "push," you neither win nor lose) on jacks-or-better. That's an outrage! Without this payout, you've lost over 20 percent in overall house percentages! It's impossible to overcome such a nasty slap in the face, so stay away from these hostile machines.

One thing is for sure. The better paytables are on the higher-priced machines. You won't find a 6-9 nickel machine, and it's even tough to find a 6-9 paytable on a quarter machine in non-competitive markets. Fifty-cent and dollar machines should give you the best percentages, but look at the paytables to be sure. If they don't, the casino you're in does not deserve the pleasure of your money.

BONUS FEATURES

The new trend today in video poker is called "bonus features." There are several popular variations, the most common of which is called "Double Bonus Deluxe." All of them have one thing in common: additional jackpots at the expense of smaller wins, usually for two pair. (You don't win at all. Your bet is only returned.) That's right. Two pair is treated the same as jacks-or-better.

These new bonus machines do have their come-ons, however. In addition to the standard royal-flush jackpot, you might find a bonus jackpot for a sequenced royal (10-J-Q-K-A, in order). Or maybe a specifically suited straight flush pays a higher jackpot. In some cases, it gets a little crazy. The paytables for four-of-kind (125 coins for five coins inserted on a standard machine) pays off at different multipliers depending on whether or not the four-of-a-kind is 2s, 3s, and 4s, or 5s through kings, or aces. If one of the smaller values hits, the five-coin win is 400 coins! You'll collect 250 coins for 5s through kings, and a whopping 800 coins for aces!

It looks good, but the cost of not getting paid your even-money win for two pair is more significant than most players think. It's all based on frequency. How many times would you expect to make two pair; how many times would you expect to make four aces? What's more, most of these bonus machines are based on 5-8 flush/full house paytables! Hmm. Players were playing them, but beginning to question the wisdom of it all. Just exactly how good are these bonus machines? It turned out that they were not as good as players thought.

Big surprise.

As a response to this growing concern among video poker players, the manufacturers have now designed better "bonus" machines that take the edge off of the "shorted" two-pair payoff by bumping up the payoff for a flush to seven coins and offering the standard machine's top full-house payoff of nine coins. This is a bonus 7-9 machine that is well worth the effort to find.

And guess what? Now the manufacturers are offering 7-10 machines in the standard configuration (without the bonus features). We're talking percentages here that rival the best bets at a craps table, on the order of only a few tenths of a percent! Low percentages, indeed!

These top-rated machines, however, are still in the minority. They are hard to find. The bulk of what you will find are 5-8 bonus and a few 6-9 standards. So remember, most of the bonus machines today give you something new but take something away. It can't come as any surprise that what it takes away is worth more than what it gives you.

It would seem as if the only complicated part of video poker is determining percentages. If all the machines were the same, then the percentages would be the same and everyone would be happy. Right? Hardly. You know as well as I do that if there were no variations in percentages, the casino industry would settle for a piece of the pie that would be far too expensive for us. That's right. The casinos would gorge themselves! We should look at the variations in percentages as a plus, a competitive element that keeps the overall playing conditions rather decent.

But for those of you who still look at percentages with a bit of skepticism, here's something else you can do that will show a machine's true colors.

A few years ago, I wrote a series of articles on game percentages and then published these articles in a book titled *How To Win!* The idea was well-received by slot players and, even today, I see players actually practicing the strategy. The concept is simple, so let me give you a précis of what it's about.

Every time you sit down to play, start with a particular denomination bill (I usually start with $20) and make sure you know the total number of plays at maximum coins that the bill will give you. With my twenty-dollar bill, for example, I know that I have 80 quarters at five quarters per play. That's 16 plays I can expect from my "buy-in."

So I play the machine 16 times. At the end of that run, I take a count of the credits on the meter. If I have more than 80 credits, the machine gave me a positive expectancy. If I have fewer than 80 credits, I was the victim of a negative expectancy. Over the long term, the machine is built on a negative expectancy, so I must keep a careful watch of the results for every 80 coins played.

I think of my play in terms of twenty-dollar sessions, but, unlike at the table games, I may very well run one session right after another, and keep running until the machine refuses to cooperate. Then it's break time while I plan for my next session at a different machine.

It's certainly arguable whether or not this tactic will lead you to more positive sessions than negative, but it does do one thing: It allows you to monitor a machine's percentages at the most important time—the time during which you're playing it!

In the *How To Win!* strategy, I provide simple formulas to compute the actual percentages. It's fun. I hope that you take it to that level. It can add a new dimension to your game plan.

Regardless of the paytables you find, you absolutely must play all five coins each and every time you play a game. It's called "play the max," and it ensures that you are in the running to win the bonus royal flush jackpot for maximum "coin in."

Remember, all payouts on a video poker machine are linear (more coins inserted only increase the win by the number of coins inserted), but the royal flush jackpot is not linear! It's at least 16 times more than the one-coin "jackpot" (250 coins). Instead of winning 1250 coins for five coins inserted, you'll win 4000! At least! It could even be considerably more in the case of progressive machines.

A word of warning, though, regarding multiple-coin machines. Don't fall victim to video poker machines that want to swallow up more than five coins per play. Generally these are gimmick machines that have multiple card images or side-pots, which are rarely worth the additional investment.

If playing five coins is too steep for you, drop down in coin value. Just as you would move up in coin value as you continue to win, simply drop down when you have to in order to be comfortable with five coins inserted. If you can only afford to play five coins on a nickel video poker machine, be advised, however, that you will not find attractive paytables.

The best paytables begin with quarters. Hopefully, quarter machines are a good starting point for you as you rack up wins and begin moving up the coin denomination ladder. It's an easy betting progression for slot players that I particularly like.

But if you've moved up to a dollar machine, and wins aren't coming in the numbers you were finding at the quarter or fifty-cent machines, drop back down in a hurry. Otherwise, you might give back your winnings in a fraction of the time it took to win it! Let common sense prevail.

There are certain strategies to follow in what cards to hold (what hands to draw to) that make playing the game as routine as using Basic Strategy at the blackjack tables. Best of all, there is one particular strategy that takes into account all of the variations in paytables. If you thought that playing video poker in the most optimum fashion was difficult, you're wrong. It's not complicated. It's fun! And armed with a powerful strategy, it can be profitable, too!

Many video poker strategies on the market today are far too conservative to result in significant short-term wins, particularly of the higher jackpots. To make sense of all this, taking the paytable variations into account, and presenting the ideal strategy for all players (called a hybrid strategy), I've published a Strategy Card on video poker that covers just about everything. It not only shows the rank of hands and the optimum paytable most likely to be found, but also the best strategy to play for those of you who want to win the bigger jackpots more frequently. For example, it's designed to increase your chances of hitting a royal flush by 20 percent! (See ad on last page of book.)

For those of you who are thinking that you have to buy something to get the strategy, you don't. Ladies and gentlemen and children of all ages (18 or over in most Indian casinos), step right up and feast your eyes on the best video poker strategy in all the world! I've always wanted to say that.

VIDEO POKER STRATEGY

YOU HAVE	DRAW
4 OF A ROYAL	1
3 OF A KIND	2
4 OF ST FLUSH	1
3 OF A ROYAL	2
2 PAIR	1
HIGH PAIR	3
4 OF A FLUSH	1
OE STRAIGHT	1
2 OF A ROYAL	3
LOW PAIR	3
CL STRAIGHT	1
3 OF ST FLUSH	2
1 HIGH CARD	4

HIGH PAIR: jacks, queens, kings, aces; LOW PAIR: 2s thru 10s. STRAIGHTS: Open end, you hold 4 consecutive cards excluding an ace; Closed, you need an inside card.

Start at the top and work down until you find your hand. Stand on straights or better, except a straight (or flush) that includes 4 of a royal.

Video poker machines, like other reel-type slot machines, can often be found in what are known as "progressive banks." The machines are electronically tied together so that the more players play, the higher the royal flush jackpot grows. It's possible that the jackpot could increase to a point where the

overall percentages actually swing to the player's favor!*

Although most video-poker progressives use 5-8 machines, you can still get the edge if the royal-flush jackpot exceeds a certain level.

Let's assume you're playing a 5-8 quarter machine, so a 4,000-coin jackpot correlates to a $1,000 win. The percentage against you on the 5-8 is higher than the 6-9 because of the short-pays for the flush and full house. But let's say we've found a 5-8 quarter progressive machine and the meter above the carousel reads $1,500. Such a significant increase in your jackpot potential eats away some of that percentage against you.

The only way you can beat the machine with a fair modicum of consistency, however, is by landing the royal. If you don't get the royal, chances are the machine will take a chunk of your money no differently from what a standard machine would do... over the long term, of course.

---

*Some progressive machines also have "add-on" jackpots, such as four aces, straight flushes, and so on. Just as the paytables can vary on a stand-alone machines, so can the jackpots (and paytables) on progressive machines.

That's why you must make your draw decisions without error. And you must play from a bankroll that can survive the ups and downs of such a valiant try.

Although there are differing opinions on how large the jackpot has to be to swing the edge in your favor on a bank of 5-8 progressive machines, I like to use the 120 percent rider as a basis for determining whether or not I want to tackle it. A 120 percent rider means the jackpot should be $2,200 on a 5-8 quarter progressive carousel. That puts us slightly ahead of the game, on paper, and we'll just have to see if we have the stamina to see it through.

The downside to this strategy is obvious. Just because the jackpot is so high, and just because you can play the hands perfectly, and even if you have an unlimited bankroll, there certainly cannot be a guarantee that you'll hit the royal. If for no other reason, some other player might hit it before *you* do! Hey, that's the chance you take. Worse yet, the likelihood is slim that you'll even find an open machine to play when the progressive jackpot is so high.

Years ago, casinos that offered progressive video poker carousels with 5-8 machines were bombarded with "professional teams" that took over all the machines when the progressive meter topped two grand. They would march in at 4 a.m., when the machines were usually sitting idle, and take them over... literally holding the machines captive. The casino's regular customers complained, and many casinos reacted by establishing stringent rules about team play. Still, it goes on, and some players do make out... like bandits.

Believe it or not, slot players need to be concerned with money management more so than table-game players. Why? Because of the speed of the machine games. But whether you're a slot player or a blackjack player, having a set of basic disciplines is crucial to your success. In a sense, it's a strategy. That's right. Basic discipline and plain common sense are perhaps the most important strategies of all!

Here are a few choice pieces of advice to help you start putting your own rules and regs together. Type them up on your computer and carry them with you every time you visit the casino. Read them before you play.

Casinos have their own rules that they follow to the letter. Professional players strictly adhere to their own unique set of rules. Casual players need their own rules, too. Win or lose, you'll feel better about yourself if you know that you played by your rules.

- **Make sure your bankroll fits your game.** Don't be under-financed. But don't be *over*-financed, either. Both of the extremes can be a problem. My advice is to find your comfort level and stick with that same bankroll amount for all of your gambling trips. If your trips vary in length, assign a certain stake per day. The key here is continuity. Drastic variations in your bankroll can have a negative effect in the way you play.

- **Do not rush to play.** Upon arrival at the casino, be prepared with something else to do first. Temper your anxiety. It might be something as simple as having breakfast or lunch, or meeting friends over coffee. Maybe you've had a long flight or a long drive. It's absolutely essential that you change gears, relax, and get in the right frame of mind before you challenge the machines.

- **Observe before you play.** There's so much
that can be gained by simply watching. Particularly if you're thinking about a certain
bank of machines. Watch the other players.
Although you can't be assured that all the machines sport the same percentages, you might
learn from watching that more walking is in
order. At the very least, judicious observing
helps you by minimizing exposure.

- **Always play the maximum number of
coins.** I've given you all the reasons why; I
can only hope I have convinced you. Remember, some machines today take more than the
typical 5-coin maximum. I've seen some machines that take up to 100 coins! Obviously,
our play-the-max rule only applies to 5-coin
machines. Watch out for the new arcade-style
10-coin machines or the new "triple"
machines that are really three machines in
one. Players tell me these machines are hard
to resist. My advice is to steer away from
"gimmick" machines of this sort and stick with
the standard 5-coin paytables.

- **Begin with relatively small bets.** Regardless of what machine price you choose,
determine your range of play and start at the

bottom. Most players have a range of 25 cents, 50 cents, and one dollar. If your range is a little lower, start with a 5-cent machine if you are fortunate enough to be playing in a casino that offers them. If you can afford to start higher, you should, because you've already learned from the preceding pages that nickel machines have the highest hold percentage of all denominations. Still, if that's all you can go, that's where you start.

- **Move up to higher machine prices as you continue to win.** At least you can utilize the advantages of a progression this way. If you've won a considerable amount on a quarter machine, move up to a 50-cent machine. If a dollar machine has filled up several buckets for you, why not try a $5-token machine in the high-roller pit? But use common sense. If the move up immediately sours, what are you going to do? You either drop back to the bottom price of your range, or quit. It's not complicated. Quitting isn't complicated.

- **Play in sessions with a specific loss limit per session.** When you reach your loss limit, the session is over. Take a break. Take a long break. Setting loss limits makes all the sense in the world. Setting win limits makes no sense at all. If you're winning, keep playing! Play as long as you win! Winning streaks come along so rarely that you must really take advantage when it happens. *Remember, always set a limit on your losses, but let your winnings run!*

- **Stay away from "Double Up" machines.** Some machines today allow you to parlay your winning wager with a "Double" feature that gives you the option of doubling a win (a double-or-nothing bet). If you lose it, you lose your winnings *and* your bet. In most cases, the house picks up a nifty 8 percent on this wager. That's an *extra* 8 percent! No strategy will work against a rip-off like that!

- **Play only those machines clearly marked "All hands dealt from 52-card deck."** Although there has been sporadic concern expressed by seasoned players lately that some machine percentages may be skewed by additional micro-processor control, I doubt the validity of those concerns, but must admit that I, too, only play machines that display the disclaimer noted. If you have been dealt three kings, you want to know that you have two shots (two cards would be discarded) at beating one in 47 odds of finding that last king. You don't want to know that there might be "additional" programming that cuts the odds of making your four-of-a-kind.

- **Avoid speeding.** Here's another item we've covered earlier. I'm sure you now know how damaging a fast game-speed can be. So slow down. Enjoy yourself. I've always believed that most players really don't want to play fast but they feel pressured to win or pressured to "get even." Everyone has internal regulators. If your biological clock simply runs too fast, let it wind down before you play. Otherwise, you might find that gambling poses a destructive conflict for you. And don't forget that a relaxed pace helps reduce long-term exposure. In any negative-expectation game, the faster (or longer) you play, the more likely you will lose.

- **Never play when you are tired or upset.** This is particularly true if you're playing a skill game such as video poker. But no matter which game you play, being tired or upset can lead to serious errors of discipline. Attitudes change when you're not sharp and alert. Why risk a serious financial setback? It will just give you something else to be upset about.

- **If you can't afford to lose it, don't bet it.** Yes, you've heard this expression before. Although it's become a worn-out cliché, I would like to restore it to its full faith and vigor. Abide by it every time you put your bankroll together, every time you reach into your wallet, and every time you make a wager.

Although this chapter is devoted to video poker, the "skill game" among slots, I want to close this chapter with a special "winning secret" for reel-type slot players, too. Players marvel at these gaudy games, the simplicity of them all, not caring much about the percentages, and rightly so, for how could they know? How could they know, indeed. Read on.

Many years ago, casinos were saddled with a myth among slot players that probably cost them millions of dollars. It was widely believed in those days that machines placed near the entrances to a casino and at the ends of aisles, or anywhere that people congregated, were the better-paying machines. The myth grew to unmanageable proportions for casino operators, when claims became even more exaggerated that certain types of machines in these locations paid out more than they held! It was said that you could identify these "special" machines by listening to the sound they made when paying out jackpots. The louder the noise, the better the payback!

Well, it was all a myth, absolutely. But here's what happened next.

Players who milked these "blessed" machines, and came away empty, assumed that all the other machines in the casino were worse. After all, if the good machines weren't, what would you expect from the rest?! Soon, the casinos got drift of the problem. It was too big to counter.

So they gave in.

Better-paying machines were actually installed in these key locations to satisfy the myth and keep the players playing *all* the machines! These "up front" machines became loss leaders, essentially, to use a retail term.

Today, there are several casinos, particularly those run by the same large corporation, that continue the practice.

So, a myth that was truly a myth became reality.

Oh, the power of slot players!

CHAPTER 6

TEXAS HOLD 'EM

The glut of poker books on the market makes it too easy to get caught up in a tangle of advice that can only end up confusing both new and experienced players. Many of these books are written by the very pros you wish to emulate.

But what I find interesting about most of them is the distinct lacking of key advice—the secrets, if you will—that, apparently, the pros just don't want you to know about. Or, perhaps, the best at the game are just a bit too presumptuous of your skills. What you'll often read are tips that fall under the categories of "Common Sense" and "I Already Know That!" Who needs it?

At the other end are the books that are plainly too complicated for even seasoned players. We all know that the pros can play. The question is: Can they teach? Can they make winners out of beginners?

I've been teaching players how to win at *all* gambling endeavors, not just poker, for nearly thirty years. I know how to play. I know how to win. But most of all, I know how to teach! So expect solid advice that *can* make winners out of beginners!

Incidentally, the worst advice I've ever read in a poker book came from a top pro: "You can't win if you don't play." Boy, is that bad advice or what?! It sends a mixed message that would be misinterpreted more often than not! "Hmm, maybe I should play this marginal hand." Maybe. Most likely not!* Here's my advice about advice: Successful playing and successful teaching are clearly two different things.

---

*In limit games and even tournament action with full or nearly full tables, amateurs tend to call too many bets; they don't fold as often as they should. At a tournament table with only head-to-head competition remaining, most hands are played to prevent the other player from stealing the blinds. As the blinds build up in later rounds, players may need to play more hands in order to stay in the game. I'll define these conditions for you as we go along in the chapter.

Before we go on to the secrets of being a winner at the poker tables, let's go over the game so that you know exactly how to play.

HOW TO PLAY THE GAME

Texas Hold 'em is played either as a "limit" game or "no limit." Most poker rooms in casinos around the country play a limit game, also referred to as a "live" game, although some tournament action can be found in even small casinos. Most tournament games, whether a low-stakes "locals" tournament or a nationally televised major tournament, are played as no limit. And there's a huge difference.

NO LIMIT HOLD 'EM

"No limit" means you can bet up to whatever you have in front of you. You can bet all of your chips if you like. It's where the commonly heard phrase, "all in," comes from. In a tournament no-limit game, you enter with a "buy-in" and are given tournament chips to play with. Winners are determined by the order of finish; you don't keep your chips and cash them in as you would in a limit game.

Your ranking as the tournament goes along is determined by what is called a "chip count." If you have two thousand dollars in chips at the end of a session, and there are 23 players with more chips than you have, you're sitting 24th, and most likely need to improve your position in order to win money. Most small tournaments pay the top 15 places. As a general rule, the more players in the tournament, the more places are paid.

As long as you have chips in front of you, you're still in the game. But, as you'll learn later on, the "forced bets"—called "blinds,"—continually grow in a no-limit game, so you can't just sit back and play only the best hands. That's the rub. And it's what makes tournament action so exciting. It's also why the same top pros are often seen at the final table in major televised tournaments. **They know how to play weak hands.** They have to know because they have to play them. Everyone does.

The growing blinds—and a diminishing number of players at the table—lend an ever-changing complexion to the game's strategy

LIMIT HOLD 'EM

A limit game, unlike no-limit tournaments, has set blinds; they don't change from the minute you sit down to the minute you walk away. The amount of the set blinds are tied in to the betting structure of a particular game.

Let's say you found a $3-$6 limit game. Although the dollar amounts suggest a range of betting—a low and high limit—it is not that at all. These dollar values represent the amounts you must wager for the four rounds of betting.

For the first two rounds, your bets must be $3. For the final two rounds, your bets must be $6. You can't bet less, but you can bet more by raising the bet. However, the raise must be the same structured amount

If a player before you bet $3, and you want to stay in the game, you have to call that player's bet by also betting $3. Depending on the strength of your hand, you might want to raise $3 (for a total of $6), which means increasing the bet to $6 for the next player to call, if that player wants to stay in the game. The player who initially bet $3 will have to toss in another $3 (when it's that player's turn again) to continue playing.

If you don't at least call a bet, you must fold your hand, which means you're out of action until the next hand.

The casino provides a dealer who actually shuffles and deals the cards, verifies the bets, settles disputes, and calls the winning hands. All poker rooms have a supervisor on duty to whom you can appeal a dealer's decision if you find yourself on the short end of a player dispute. Hey, it happens.

Since there's significant "position" advantage as to where you sit in relation to the dealer, each player takes a turn acting as dealer. A dealer "button" rotates around the table in a clockwise direction to mark this important spot at the table. The player with the dealer button is the last to play; meaning that player can weigh all the actions of the other players before acting on his or her own hand.

The two players directly left of the player "on the button" are in tough spots, however, since it's their responsibility to get the engine running by posting the blinds for the first round of betting. (The blinds are posted for the first betting round only.)

POSTING THE BLINDS

Before the dealer begins, both players directly left of the dealer button are required to make these two forced bets. The first player to the left makes a bet called the "small blind." The player

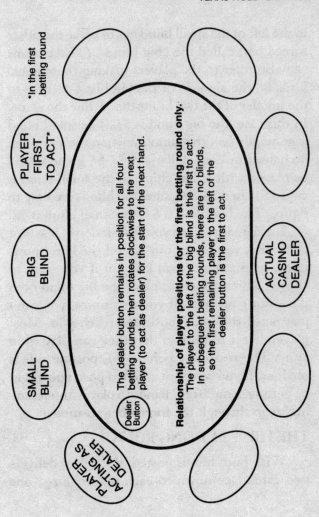

*In the first betting round

PLAYER FIRST TO ACT*

BIG BLIND

SMALL BLIND

PLAYER ACTING AS DEALER

Dealer Button

ACTUAL CASINO DEALER

The dealer button remains in position for all four betting rounds, then rotates clockwise to the next player (to act as dealer) for the start of the next hand.

Relationship of player positions for the first betting round only.
The player to the left of the big blind is the first to act. In subsequent betting rounds, there are no blinds, so the first remaining player to the left of the dealer button is the first to act.

to the left of the small blind has to make the other forced bet, called the "big blind." (These terms can also refer to the players making these bets.) Usually, the amount of the big blind is equal to the smaller of the two limits that define the game. In this case, the big blind is $3. The small blind is generally half that amount when the value can be halved in even dollars. A $3-$6 game would be played with dollar chips, so the small blind is cut to $1. In a $4-$8 game, the blinds are easy to figure. The big blind is $4, the small blind is $2.

Incidentally, when you first sit down, it's most likely that you are not in one of the blind positions, so the dealer will ask you if you want to "post," which means to place the big blind even if it's not your turn. If you don't post, you can't play until the blind positions reach you. Most players elect to post so that they can play right away. The reasoning behind this posting rule is obvious. If you were not asked to post, you might be getting some "free" hands to play without having to go through the forced bet positions.

THE FIRST BETTING ROUND

With both blinds posted, the dealer delivers two cards face-down to each player. First, one card goes to each player and then the second card is dealt to each player. These two cards are your "hole" cards, also called "pocket" cards, and they are for your eyes only. Be careful how you view your hole cards since you might have players sitting directly beside you.

Most players like to pull their cards close to the edge of the table (but not off the table) with the long way of the cards running away from them. Then, they slide them apart just enough to be able to see both card values as they bend the top edges of the cards upward with their thumbs while cupping the cards with their hands. The card values are flashed for just an instant. **It's interesting to note that players who take too long to look are usually signaling off-suited cards (cards of different suits).**

The player to the left of the big blind is first to act, and must decide whether to call the big blind (match the $3 bet), raise to $6, or fold.

The next player goes through these same options, then the next, and so on, until the betting gets around to the small blind. If the small blind wants to stay in the game, another $2 needs to be wagered. (Remember, the small blind is in for $1; the big blind is in for $3.) Unless there was a raise along the way, the small blind is essentially calling the big blind's $3.

Incidentally, your bets are not tossed onto the table in some reckless fashion, but placed directly in front of you, maybe a foot or so out onto the table. After all players have acted, the bets are gathered in by the dealer, creating a "pot" in the near-center of the table.

THE SECOND BETTING ROUND: THE FLOP

The dealer begins the second betting round by "flopping" (placing) three cards in the center of the table face-up. These cards are the first three of five "community cards" that all players can use—along with their pocket cards—to make the best poker hand.

Betting begins with the first active player to the left of the dealer button. There are no more blinds to contend with. And some players likely folded during the first round, so there are probably fewer players to contend with.

The first player to bet in this second round has an additional betting option that wasn't available in the first round: to "check," which means to pass. A player could not check in the first round because of the blinds. You can't check a bet. You can only check if no one has bet before you.

Because many players in a "cheap" game ($3-$6 certainly qualifies as cheap) usually stay in the game to see the flop, regardless of the strength of their pocket cards, this betting round generally sees the most folds. If the flop didn't help, well, it only cost a few bucks. That's their logic. And it's a dangerous notion. Those "few bucks" will eat them up in short order with that kind of ill-advised reasoning. But they came to play, and play they do.

THE THIRD BETTING ROUND: THE TURN

The pivotal third round begins with the dealer placing a fourth community card on the table, called the "turn card." What's significant about this round is the increase in the betting limit. In our theoretical $3-$6 game, all bets are now $6, not $3 as in the first two rounds. So, if the first active player left of the button tosses in $6, and the next player raises $6, now it's up to you to call $12 if you want to stay in the game.

Serious money? If a $3-$6 game is your speed, yes, $12 is serious. But hear me out on this.

Money values are relative, I know. But why wait until the third round to take it seriously? Sadly, it's the way many rookie players play the game. If that $6 raise spooked you, you might want to search out a $2-$4 game. Better yet, I suggest you rack up experience and learn from it, develop the street smarts and basic book knowledge so that you can find the confidence to play at *higher* limits, not lower… for serious money!

THE FOURTH BETTING ROUND: THE RIVER

The fourth and final round of betting starts with the dealer placing a fifth card directly beside the turn card. This card, called the "river card," will pretty much tell you whether it's time to go for the jugular or limp out of the game.

And that's a rather accurate appraisal of your choices because, at this stage of the game, you're virtually assured of significant betting action. You've gauged the possible hands of your opponents. Hopefully, you've got a good read on them, too. But more often than not, it's a fight to the finish with only those players holding strong hands. As I alluded to earlier, **there's little bluffing in a "cheap" game, so be prepared for battle.**

After the betting is completed, there is a showdown if more than one player remains. But if one player bounced all the others out of the game, there is no showing of the cards. The winning player would be foolish to do so.

TYPICAL $3-$6 LIMIT HOLD 'EM FORMAT

BETTING ROUND	CARDS DEALT	BET/RAISE AMOUNT	BLINDS
1	2 (Pocket)	$3	$1/$3
2	3 (Flop)	$3	—
3	1 (Turn)	$6	—
4	1 (River)	$6	—

BEYOND THE BASICS

"Things may come to those who wait, but only the things left by those who hustle."

-Abraham Lincoln

As important as patience is, don't confuse it with being timid. There's great value in patience; sometimes you just need to bide your time. But when the time comes, you need to "hustle," you need to find your aggression knob and turn it up.

You can't let a fear of losing keep you out of a decent hand. Yet I see it all the time, particularly when the blinds begin to build at a no-limit game. If you're the timid type, poker is not your game.

Knowing when to turn up the attack and when to lay back is what separates the pros from the wannabes. And it's not just about poker. This rare trait is a hallmark of success in any competition.

Before you play, take every opportunity to size up the other players; get a read on any quirks in a particular player's betting habits. The tendency for most players is not to change their style, so what you might learn from these precious few minutes can work for you over a potentially long session at the table.

Earlier, I mentioned that the dealer will ask new players at a limit game if they want to post. If you recall, the idea is to prevent a new player from enjoying a few "free" hands without having to post the blinds. Players who answer "yes" can play immediately. Players who answer "no" must wait until the blinds reach their position at the table.

And that's just fine. A little time to unwind— after all, you just sat down—but more important, a little time to watch the other players play poker. You would be surprised how much you can pick up in just a short time.

In the days when I played frequently in downtown Las Vegas casinos (my favorite stomping grounds), I remember a player who would always buy in, sit down (there was rarely a wait in those days), and then just study the players before he even stacked his chips. He might sit out half-a-dozen hands before he played, but he was up to the table, and he was making his presence felt. Can you relate to this tactic?

Everyone got to know him since he was a regular, so to speak, among so many other regulars, but there was always a fresh face or two to study. Always. And this particular player, who would become a star player on tour decades later, would tend to rile these new players with the way he would stare them down.

One of the many quotes from this great player that I'll never forget is a good way to end this piece: "People think that poker is a game of luck and skill. Well, more than that, it's a game of remembering. I never forget faces, I never forget names, and I can tell you everything you need to know to beat those players. Because I know every little telling habit they have. I store it all away; I never forget."

The concept of getting reads on other players is fundamental to poker. Of course, this is a two-pronged attack. You must learn how to develop your own mystique, too. And, of vital importance, jam the airwaves when other players try to tune you in.

The idea, of course, is to get a read on *them*, but not let them get a read on *you*. Players who won't let other players penetrate their shields are ahead of the game. You want to be a mystery to other players. You want to frustrate them. Try to become an unpredictable, hard-to-read combatant; mix up your actions well enough that no one has an inkling whether you have rockets in your pocket or 10s that need a booster.

My old poker buddy who I quoted earlier is deserving of another quote: "When I stare down other players, I'm careful to make it a one-way street. I want to get inside their heads, but I don't want them to get inside mine!"

Few poker players without this psychological edge are successful. It's that simple. So how do you see through the other players' masks; how do you hide behind yours?

A key question. It deserves a key answer.

What has made televised poker tournaments so successful is the concept of showing the viewers the players' hole cards. It's a clever idea that, without it, would probably have relegated poker tournaments on TV to the ratings of hot-dog eating contests. Knowing all the hole cards makes TV viewers think they're more of an expert than they are. But it makes it all the more exciting.

What they may not know is that some players might as well have a TV monitor right on the table in front of them. That's right. It's remarkable what some players can discern through sheer observation. Subtle movements made by players can indicate the strength, or weakness, of their hands. Most rookie players overly exhibit these "tells" in the act of bluffing, which is why few can successfully pull it off. But tells can be read at any time. Do your eyes light up when you see the card you need? Or does your chin drop when you *don't* get the right card?

Many of the pros learned about their own tells by having other pros watch them. It's hard for most players to detect their own tells. Some will even go to the extreme of video taping a mock session. It's common practice for pros who play on TV to tape the programs to not only look for other players' tells, but for their own, too.

If you don't have the opportunity... yet... to tape yourself on a televised tournament, then go ahead and tape a mock session with your friends. Study the tape over and over. You'll be surprised how many easy tells are there for the picking. Whether you study a tape or a player at a live game, this experience can only build in your favor.

Let's close this piece with an often-heard comment about detecting tells. Many top players believe that this critical attribute is an innate quality, not a learned skill. But I find that comment highly suspect. It's arguable, but I personally believe that the skill *can* be developed, and I've always recommended that poker buddies get together and instead of just playing around for a few bucks, actually spend some time working on tell detection. That's right. Work with your friends to hone your skills.

The pros do it. So why don't you try it? The players who are really into physical analysis tend to perform better, regardless. That's a fact. One player in particular who I used to play with claimed that he had worked on it for so long that he developed a new sense (would that be the sixth?) and it not only helped him in poker but in his business world, too. He called it "super-vision," and he called upon it often: Is that guy telling the truth? Does he really have a better offer? Is that the best price I can get?

With all the psychological edges you can muster, and with all the knowledge you may have accumulated, it's still darn tough to beat a good table if you don't get the cards. You need good cards. Let's not dance around it! I don't care how good you are, if it's just not your day, you're going to get beat.

Knowing how to deal with adversity is the mark of a successful player. Many players, experienced or not, don't have a clue.

The typical response is to keep pulling the trigger when they're out of bullets. Click, click, click. When you're out of ammo, the smartest thing to do is to holster your weapon and retreat. Go plan for the next battle. There will always be a "next time."

For those of you who are relatively new to the game, I'll confirm for you what you want to see in the pocket: aces and face cards. You want to see lots of paint! And if you're not getting those good cards, there's no book in the world that can help you. If you're stuck in a no-limit game, you better hope the session ends soon and hope for a better tomorrow. If you're in a limit game, the answer's easy. Rise from your chair, say "Good day, gentlemen," and *wait* for a better tomorrow.*

Do you play golf? If you do, then that's a good way to play out your day. But you'll probably shoot a horrible round because, well, a bad day is a bad day. We all have them. The key is how we deal with them.

One of my favorite gambling expressions is, "You can't force the cards." Sure, you can try to outfox the other players with weak hands but that won't get you through the day. How nice it would be if you knew what you were getting into before you plunked down your money.

A smattering of top players I know seem to have a strangely instinctive, intuitive sense about their day over that first cup of coffee. Call it pre-monition, call it timing, call it whatever you want to, but I give tons of credit to those rare players who have such a keen sense of awareness. Simply put, they know *when* to play. They know when *not* to play.

---

*The "Rank of Poker Hands" chart appears on page 141.

The key strategy of Texas Hold 'em, whether a limit or no-limit game, is knowing the relative values of your pocket cards. And the values *are* relative. The worth of your hand is always relative to the conditions at a particular table at a particular time. Never think of pocket card values as absolutes.

Clearly, it would be difficult to put together a list of pocket-card values, for the reasons cited. And there are more reasons that we'll get to later in the chapter. Still, I've found that rank beginners need such a list. In fact, they demand it. I guess they just feel more comfortable with it. Whatever the reason, I've listed pocket-card values in the following chart. Beginners will gain more from it as it relates to full or near-full tables.

The chart includes all the hands, in relative order of strength, from a J-10 and up. But remember what we just learned. These values are not cut in stone. Your standing, the number of players, the overall strength of these players, and particularly their real-time actions, all affect your decisions to play or fold even the relatively strong hands that I've listed.

It's why the game is called poker, and not blackjack, where absolutes abound. But not at the poker tables. No, it's a thinking game. And most times, what pro players are thinking about is whether or not they want to buck the "absolutes," or even cuddle up to a relatively weak hand. It's what makes the game so... unpredictable.

To the extent that you can break through a player's facade of unpredictability, you have acquired an edge.

BEST CARDS IN THE POCKET
(IN DESCENDING ORDER, READING DOWN)

GROUP 1	GROUP 2	GROUP 3
A-A	J-J	K-J
K-K	K-Q	K-10
A-K	A-J	Q-J
Q-Q	10-10	Q-10
A-Q	A-10	J-10

Notes: If the unpaired hands are suited, it's an obvious plus. Surprisingly, however, the rank does not change significantly whether suited or off-suit, in these higher-value cards.

Since many players in a limit game routinely stay in to see the flop, this habit tends to skew our pocket-card values. The same can be said for the fewer number of head-to-head contests compared to a tournament game. As you can now appreciate, pocket card values are essentially empirical, and often debated. There are simply too many variables to assign absolute ranking.

There is a general progression among these top 15 hands, although it is a mild one indeed. In theory, the first group of pocket cards is your best ammo for any number of players, of any strength. Fire away!

The second group would seem to be the same, but holding 10-10 against a full table of top players might make you think, and it should. Against four or five players, top-guns or not, it's a different story. Play 'em!

The third group, all strong hands, too, are usually a green light against three or four players. But remember, you might also want to fire them off against a full table, depending on the composition of players.

TOP PLAYERS KNOW THE VARIABLES AND APPLY THEM IN TERMS OF ODDS, NOT ABSOLUTES

There are three main factors that impact on pocket-card strength: (1) the likelihood of getting beat with an overcard,* (2) the high value of your cards, and (3) the number of players in the game. Let's discuss these factors one at a time:

---

*An overcard is any community card higher in value than both of your hole cards.

1. Overcard vulnerability. Let's say you're holding a pair of 6s, certainly not a strong hand, even though pairs are always tempting to play. It's likely that several players, at a full or nearly full table, will have at least one card in their pockets that's higher than a 6. That card could easily pair up with the overcard and beat you. You have to survive five shots (the five community cards) at beating your lowly 6s. The only community card that could improve your hand is another 6.*

Of course, there's always the likelihood that another player at a full table holds a higher pair. If the community cards don't help you—and it's unlikely they would—you're beaten right out of the gate.

The only real hope with such a marginal hand is that other players do not pair up, or, if they do, they pair below your 6s. That's a lot to hope for.

2. High-value strength. Obviously, an ace is the best card to have in your pocket. If the other card is also high—let's say it's a king—that's even bet-

---

*In a head-to-head tournament game (against one other player), it's a totally different story. Your low pair might be top hand! After all, you only have one other hand to beat, not eight or nine, so you are in a decent position.

ter. If the other card is also an ace, you've got the best possible hole cards.

But, if you stay in with a 5 and 6 off-suit (of different suits), these are certainly not high cards and are easily beat. Your only hope is to make two pair or get real lucky and fill a straight. If the 5 and 6 are suited (of the same suit), that does change the complexion of your hand since a flush also becomes a possibility. Making flush draws, however, or attempting to fill straights, should not be first on your list. You are first interested in numerical values, a more likely contributor to a win.

3. Number and quality of players. As the number of active players decreases, you have fewer chances of getting beat by a lucky draw. You can often make the assumption at a full table that some other player has a stronger hand than you do, but you certainly cannot make that assumption at a short table. The fewer the players, the fewer the shots taken at you.

Whenever a game is played short, the value of pocket cards changes dramatically. At a full table, I'll toss 9-10 suited, but I might play it in a short limit game; it's a definite go if the blinds are building and players are thinning out in a no-limit tournament. You don't necessarily need the big guns to beat half an army.

A further consideration to pocket-card valuation is based on the type of game you're playing—limit or no-limit—and the inherent idiosyncrasies of these two distinctly different ways of playing the game. Let's take each separately:

LIMIT GAME. Are you playing in a low-stakes or high-stakes game? Remember, players in a low-stakes game tend to play out their hands, so there is rarely any real playing strategy to contend with. The best hand wins. It's often that simple.

Higher limit games, such as $10-$20, can be won or lost on sound betting strategies, even with somewhat weaker hands, if you know how to hide your weakness.

Make other players make mistakes. Make them fold when they should stay, and stay when they should fold.

To do this, take control of the game. Most players don't raise as often as they should, so instead of calling, as you might often do, raise instead and take control.

The quality of players is of significant importance to hand valuation in a limit game. Are you up against good players or beginners? Surprisingly, this is not usually a consideration in a no-limit game, particularly a high buy-in tournament, because you can fairly assume that all players are good. Maybe *too* good.

My choice has always been a progression of limit games, starting with $5-$10 and moving up through $10-$20 and perhaps to $20-$40 if my success continues. The varying quality of players I run into along the way is quite remarkable. A key to winning is how quickly I can discern the other players' abilities.

NO-LIMIT GAME. The escalating price of the blinds can have a huge impact on the hands you play. Until the blinds become significant, however, play in the same manner as you would a higher-priced limit game. For many players, this means a conservative approach, both in the hands they play and the way they play them. Such players are keyed to two things: staying in the game, and building up rations.

As the blinds increase, you'll reach the point where you will have to play weak hands to remain in the game. And it's always late in the game when the best players make their moves. You may find yourself in a heated head-to-head battle, playing nearly every hand just to prevent the other player from stealing the blinds (winning the blinds because the other player folded).

Remember what I said earlier. The reason you see many of the same pros at numerous final tables is because they know how to play weak hands. Skillful bluffs are the obvious edge, but getting a read on the other players is just as important. And don't think that luck doesn't count, either; players will take all they can get!

It's interesting to note that many of the non-professionals who make it into the later rounds will often switch gears to an ultra-conservative strategy. Sensing that they are close to finishing "in the money," they tend to play as if they're in a cheap limit game, tossing away the best of the weak hands. With a dwindling stake, they've already committed themselves to 15th place and a small piece of the cash prize.

Not the attitude of a winner!

In either a limit or no-limit game, don't play for just a flush or a straight. Players tend to overvalue suited pocket cards unless they are high cards. Most hands are won on high

pairs, two pairs, or trips (three-of-a-kind). With fewer players, many hands are won on just high card. You should always make this fact a key consideration in evaluating your pocket cards.

But, as we've talked about in the case of no-limit games, sometimes you have to play tough hands. A good poker player can rank these hands; tough hands are certainly not all the same.

For example, 2-3 suited compared to 6-7 suited is weaker on two counts. For the obvious reason, the card values are smaller. For another, there is a better chance of making a straight with a 6-7, even though making a straight should be a secondary consideration.

The weaker 2-3 will only team up with a 4-5-6 or A-4-5, whereas the 6-7 can team up with 3-4-5, 4-5-8, 5-8-9, or 8-9-10.

It's worth noting that many tough hands don't even give you the possibility of a straight draw. A hand of 4-10, for example, won't make it the easy way (using both pocket cards) because there's too big of a gap between the card values. The thin straight possibilities you have only allow you to use one of your pocket cards. You would need to get lucky with, say, J-Q-K-A on the board! Fat chance!

With a hand like 4-10 off-suit, you can only hope to pair up, preferably with another 10, but a better "hope" is that the other players left in the game have hands just as shaky as yours!

There's no question about it. Being forced to play tough hands is the gamble of no-limit Hold 'em.

The Number One fault of most beginners is a failure to fold. Beginners simply call too many bets. Folding, particularly during the early betting rounds, is tough for some players to do because... well, because they came to play. They don't want to just sit there watching other players play.

In the later rounds, these amateur players have a different excuse for not folding. They've stuck around for most of the game, made an investment they hate to walk away from, and actually feel obligated to stay in the fight. But poker isn't a boxing match, it's a game of strategy. Sure, there's always the hope of catching the right card on the river, but poker isn't won on hope, it's won on skill... and discipline. The discipline to play three hands, maybe four, out of ten.

Besides, there's plenty to do if you're out of a game. And I don't mean play with your chips. Work on studying the other players. You'll get a different sense of their playing habits when you're only observing instead of participating.

If you're still chewing on my mention of playing three or four hands out of ten, folding 60 to 70 percent of the time, let me give you some hard facts:

The statistics on folding in major tournaments versus small, regional tournaments is rather telling. Nearly 70 percent of the hands in the early rounds of big tournaments (against full tables) are folded. Yet, only 50 percent of the early-round hands are tossed in smaller tournaments. I don't know the statistic for low-stakes limit games, but I'm willing to bet that it's no more than 40 percent. According to those who keep watch over the actions of professional players, 65 to 70 percent of hands folded is about right.

So what does that say for the average players? It says that they go to the poker rooms of casinos across the country to play. Winning, apparently, is secondary.

TESTING THE DECK

Top players today would be happy to tell you what they did during the days when they were just starting out. They practiced. And what they wanted to learn more than anything else was how to get a good feel for pocket-card values.

They dealt out hand after hand to see how each would play out. You should do the same. And here's your first assignment: Find out the relative strength (referring back to our Pocket Card Value Chart) of 10-10 vs. J-10. Test each of these two hands against a full table and against one other player as if in head-on competition. And then test them against each other.

Make sure all the cards are face up so that you're seeing the dynamics of the hands as they play out. You might be surprised to note the strength of high-value overcards and the frequency with which they can beat your pair of 10s. If you run enough test hands, you should come out of the "practice" with greater respect for your 10s. Pairs have power.

But so do overcards! If I'm playing 10s, and I see two overcards on the flop, it's doubtful I'll see the turn card unless the gods of chance graced me with another 10.

Poker tournaments today are filled with excitement… and noise. It's a remarkable change from the early days of poker when the game was treated as if it were a golf match. **Play the game with total concentration. Don't look around the room. Who cares what's out there? The action is right in front of you! Keep any interference at bay.** And while you're at it, learn how to psych yourself up for a big game, even if it isn't that big. You'll play better!

Top poker players, particularly those from the old school, have a knack for tuning out the din of a noisy poker room. It's not chess, but there's a considerable amount of strategy required. There's plenty to think about, much to remember, and certainly some tough decisions to make.

Here's a quote I'll always remember from a poker pro who said it best:

"All I think about is poker. Even before the game, I'm playing back old hands, recalling the players, the right moves, the wrong moves… all to get me in the right gear: Forward! At the table, you could light a firecracker behind me and I wouldn't hear it. Poker. That's all I'm thinking about when the chips are down."

Poker room managers know the games inside and out. Their wisdom in understanding the right moves at the Hold 'em tables and their willingness to help new players are highlighted in the following tips from many of the top poker room managers across the country. Heed their advice.

New players don't protect their hands. They either forget to, or they don't know how. Put your hand on the table directly in front of you and protect it with a chip marker (one of your chips) placed on top of your cards. **Otherwise, if another player throws his cards away and they land on your cards, you have a dead hand.**

Vito, poker room supervisor,
Ameristar Casino, Kansas City, MO.

Betting out of turn is a problem I see. By jumping ahead, a player could force someone to fold. And some players do it on purpose to intimidate a player to drop out of the game. Something else beginners should know: **A card dropped on the floor is dead.** Drop 'em both, you lose 'em both. Technically, you're not out of the game, you can still play the flop, but why?

Ray, pit manager,
Bally's, Atlantic City, NJ.

If a player needs to leave the table to eat, we give up to 30 minutes. But for any other reason our rules are a little different: If the button goes around the table three times, we page. If the player doesn't answer, the seat is given up. **When a player takes a break, the player's chips must stay on the table. If the chips are picked up, the player has lost his seat.** We're "table stakes" here. So taking stakes off the table ends the play. We're also very personalized with players, having only five tables. I always suggest that beginners find a smaller room like ours where they can be helped their first time out.

> Dick, poker room supervisor,
> Atlantis Casino, Reno, NV.

Poker is like an investment. Always protect your investment—your cards *and* your money—by managing it wisely. Only play the best value hands, either in live games (limit Hold 'em) or even no-limit, where the blinds can sometimes force you to play weaker hands. But, depending on how much you have in front of you in a no-limit game, you can still bet value hands much of the time. And **know the players you're going**

up against, especially if your "best value hand" is weaker than you would like.

> Eric, poker room manager,
> Arizona Charlies, Las Vegas, NV.

I see it all the time: Beginners, even veterans, complain that they're running bad, and they blame it on bad luck. So I pose this question to them: Are you sure you're good enough? Maybe you need to improve your game... statistics, emotions, the psychological part of the game. **If you continually lose, don't try to convince yourself you're just unlucky.** That's a dangerous cop-out. You're kidding yourself. You need a certain temperament, a certain discipline for gambling. And you need patience. Do you have these qualities?

> Kamell, poker room shift manager,
> Bellagio, Las Vegas, NV

Most beginners show a tendency to want to play too many hands. My advice: Be conservative. At a low-limit game, good starting hands are paramount because it's hard to bluff. In the long run, better players win because they play better starting hands. Incidentally, **the worst hand is**

2-7 off-suit, the lowest hand (without an ace) with no straight possibilities. The worst starting hand is hard to say... depends on the game, who's in the game, whether you're winning or losing. Tell your readers to keep records of results of play of certain hands, and win/loss records, too. You can really learn from your notes.

Jack, poker lead floor,
Bicycle Casino, Bell Garden, CA.

Patience is most important. **New players think two bucks isn't much; next thing you know, you're "two-bucked" to death.** It's frustrating in low-limit games that everyone plays out their cards, so you better wait for a good hand. We get better players at 4-8, but you know what? You still need good hands. I tell beginners that just because you have two suited cards, two hearts for example, it doesn't necessarily mean it's a good hand. It's interesting to note, too, that we have six tables going, and they're all Texas Hold 'em. A couple of stud games might go, but everyone wants to play Hold 'em!

Deanna, poker room manager,
Cactus Pete's, Jackpot, NV

To play in a small tournament is better than a limit game for beginners because you get to start with more chips. For a $35-buy-in, players get $1,500 in chips and valuable experience that could last for several sessions. Playing with your own money at a limit game could end up costing a player many times that amount. Our $35-buy-in tournaments have five tables, that's 55 players (11 players at a table), and we pay the top four places. Bigger tournaments, like our $100-buy-in, pays 15 places.

Brenda, pit manager,
Chinook Winds Casino, Lincoln City, OR

There's nothing more fun than pushing out all of your chips and doubling up in a tournament game. We do a lot of $25-buy-in, no-limit tournaments which get you a thousand in chips. A ten-dollar "re-buy" gets you another thousand. Tournaments last about five hours and are much different from a "structured" limit game. My advice: **During the first three or four rounds, hang low... tournaments are a process of elimination, so let the field bust each other out.** Then the cream comes to the top and you have to start playing some good poker. Don't get caught up in burning off your chips early.

James, poker room manager,
Colorado Belle Casino, Laughlin, NV

First, get a Texas Hold 'em computer game; play on that for a while because it's the easiest way to learn without losing money. Then, once you feel comfortable with the game, go to a casino and play in a live game, a low-limit game like 2-4. Or, try a 1-2 blind, no-limit Hold 'em game because that's what everyone's looking for. There are no betting limits, but you only have to start with a $2 call of the big blind. It's the same action of a big tournament, but no big risk. It's table stakes, minimum buy-in is $50, most players go in for $100 to $200. Low-limit tournaments, no-limit action, are good for beginners, too. Internet gambling is OK, but get experience first on the computer game.

Brad, acting day-shift supervisor,
Gold Strike Casino, Tunica, MS

Players come in expecting a no-limit game, that's all they see on TV, but we have a lot of structured limit games too, occasionally a no-limit game, or a pot-limit game (where you can bet up to what's in the pot). We get some players who try 7-card stud games, but mostly the beginners want Texas Hold 'em because it's faster, a lot of action, and it's what they see on TV. Some beginners, though, who sit down at a stud game, like it. They have to play their own hand, and they like that. My advice, though, is to play what you're looking for; **don't try a different game you might not know just because a seat's open.**

Alberto, Poker room supervisor,
Harrah's East Chicago Casino,
East Chicago, IN.

Believe it or not, we see players come in who don't even know the ranking of the hands. They don't know what hands to play or fold. They're coming here prematurely; every day we have to help teach these beginners how to play, and we don't mind doing that at all. TV tournaments sometimes give new players the wrong impression... the misbehavior of some pros, for example, is the worst thing. **Players need to know game etiquette.** They can't run around the tables and act like kids. They want to be like the pros, but sometimes we have to calm them down.

Doc, Poker room supervisor,
The Nugget, Sparks, NV

Incidentally, many of the poker room managers I talked to couldn't believe the number of new players who walk in with a completely distorted view of the rules of the game. They've been playing in private games with their friends, making up a lot of their own rules, and then they step into a structured casino game and feel totally lost.

Speaking for many of the poker experts, the advice is clear: Learn the game from the outset the *right* way. And even though all the managers I spoke with indicated that they are more than happy to help out beginners, it's clearly incumbent on all new players to learn the game first, maybe practicing on a computer game as one manager mentioned, and, perhaps most important, forging an intimate relationship with a good poker book.

Experience in a live game is an absolute must. But first, get the knowledge you need to make the most of that experience.

THE LANGUAGE OF POKER

If you're going to play Hold 'em, you should learn the terms that are commonly used. Poker has its own language. If you use the wrong terms, or ask what a particular term means, you're giving yourself away as a rookie.

Accordingly, I've done more in this chapter than just define the terms. I've elaborated on many of them so that you fully understand not only what they mean, but how to use them.

Ace kicker: A hand that includes an ace and a pair.

Ace-high: (1) A hand that includes an ace, but no pair or better. (2) A straight, flush, or straight flush with an ace serving as the highest card in the hand.

Aces up: A hand that includes two pairs, one of which is two aces.

Action: (1) A term used in all gambling endeavors to mean simply "in the game," (in action). (2) The term can also mean the amount or degree of betting ("The action was furious!")

Advertise: (1) A deceptive practice of bluffing with the intention of showing your weak hand. (2) Any intentional action on the part of a good player to suggest inexperience.

All the way: In a table-stakes game, a dealer will announce "all the way" when all players are all-in and all betting rounds have not been completed. The remaining rounds will be dealt "all the way" through since no betting is possible.

All-in: A situation where all of a player's money is in the pot.

Ante: A bet made by all players before the cards are dealt to ensure action. (2) The term can also refer to the number of chips or amount of money to make up the ante. (3) The term can also refer to the procedural aspect of making this bet.

Back in: Similar to a check-and-raise, a player "comes back into the betting" after first checking. Usually, the player simply calls a bet or raises. If the player raises, the action is a "check and raise." Both motives are somewhat deceptive because the player is assumed to be holding a decent hand. But it could be a ruse.

Backdoor: In general, a backdoor refers to a hand that a player was not trying to make. Usually, the backdoor hand is a flush or straight when the player, at the outset, appeared destined for a high pair, maybe two pair, at best. Most often, the better hand is made on the last two deals.

Bad beat: The act of getting beat with a strong hand… by a stronger hand. Not a fun thing. The only consolation is a chance to win a bad-beat jackpot that many casinos offer. And I'm not talking boobie prizes. Some casinos offer seats in big tournaments in lieu of cash prizes.

Bankroll: The money that poker players carry for the purpose of buying into games. Seasoned players think of each buy-in as a "session," which may end early or late, depending on the player's fortunes. To protect a bankroll, smart gamblers set a loss limit for each session. It's not wise, however, to set limits on your winnings, being careful not to play your winnings into losses.

Belly buster: Sometimes called a "gutshot," these terms refer to a player's hope of filling an inside straight. For example, if a player's pocket cards are 10-J, and the 7 and 8 are "on the board," only a 9 will "fill" the straight.

Big blind: (1) A forced bet (to ensure action) made by the player who is two positions left of the dealer button. The big blind is posted (made) before any cards are dealt. In limit games, the amount of this bet is usually the lower of the two betting limits. In a $4-$8 game, the big blind is $4. (2) The term may also refer to the player who is in that position.

Big Slick: Pocket cards of A-K, the third strongest hand behind A-A and K-K.

Blank: A card of no value to a player.

Blinds: See "big blind" or "small blind."

Bluff: A deceptive maneuver whereby a player bets on a weak hand as if the hand is strong. Bluffs are rarely used in low-limit games because the stakes are not high enough to make other players ponder the risk of staying in the game.

Board: (1) Another term for the "community cards" placed face up in the middle of the table for all players to use. (2) The center area of the table where the community cards are placed.

Boat: A shortened version of "full boat," a slang term for "full house" such as three 9s and two kings.

Bring it in: To start the betting. In the first betting round, the third player to the left of the dealer button is the first to have the option of betting.

Burn: To remove a card or cards from the top of the deck by a dealer before any cards are dealt to the players or to the board.

Button: A small plastic disk usually with the word *Dealer* printed across, used in games where a casino dealer is employed, and player position relative to the dealer is significant. The button rotates clockwise around the table after each hand so that all players can "act" as the dealer, thus allowing all players to experience all betting positions.

Buy the card: To call a bet simply because you want to see the next card.

Buy-in: (1) The establishment of a stake, almost always in chips, at the beginning of, and specifically for, a particular game. The term is easily confused with "bankroll." A buy-in is generally much less than a player's total bankroll for the session. (2) Casinos also use the term *buy-in* to mean the cost for entering a tournament.

Call: Making a bet equal to a previous player's bet. If a player elects not to call, or raise, the only other option is to fold the hand.

Cards speak: A rule typical of all card rooms to protect players from announcing their hands incorrectly. Dealers are always on the alert to make sure a hand is what the player says it is. Most often, a player who makes an incorrect announcement has overlooked a higher hand. The highest hand is played, regardless of how a player announced it.

Cash out: To quit a game and then cash in your chips. Of all the disciplines to follow, cashing out at the right time should be high on your list; but it's low on the list of reckless players.

Chase: Players are "chasing the cards" when they suspect that another player(s) has a better hand but they continue in the game in the hope of drawing the right cards against steep odds.

Check-raise: To check and later raise within the same betting round. Of course, in order to raise, another player must bet after you've checked. A player who plans to check and raise, usually with a strong hand, is "milking" other players into the pot and then bumping them up more. It's a sly tactic that is not allowed in some games.

Check: (1) To check is not to bet. Beginning with the second betting round, a player can check when first to act or if previous players have checked. (2) A "check" is casino parlance for "chip."

Close to the chest: (1) Timid, conservative betting. (2) A fear among many players that other players might have seen their cards. Thus, such players would hold their cards "close to the chest." Now a cliche.

Community cards: The five cards dealt face up to the middle of the table that may be used by all players in making their best hands.

Chip: A 1–5/8" round plastic disk that serves as cash at the tables. They come in various color-coded denominations. Chips are used because they are easier to work with than cash. The problem, however, is that chips tend to distort values, looking more like play-money than *real* money.

Connectors: Pocket cards with adjacent values, such as 9-10. Suited connectors, of course, means the cards are of the same suit.

Consolidation of tables: In most tournaments, when the number of remaining players dwindles, the tables are "consolidated" in order to expedite the run to the final table. This saves dealer expenses and helps to confine the action to fewer tables as the tournament progresses.

Cowboys: A slang term for kings.

Deuce: A slang term for a 2, also known as "2-spot."

Draw out: Making a winning hand out of a so-so hand, usually with the last card.

Drawing dead: A predicament whereby a player can't possibly win the hand, regardless of the draw.

Ducks: Casino jargon for a pair of 2s in the pocket. (Not to mention a pair of 2s at the dice table—a hard 4.)

Dump: To fold a hand.

Early position: Usually one of the first three betting positions (after the blinds in the first betting round).

Fifth Street: The last community card; also known as "the river."

Flop: The first three community cards, dealt all at once in the second betting round. Also used as a verb: "The dealer flopped a queen-ace-6."

Flush: Any five cards of the same suit.

Fold: To drop out of a hand by surrendering your cards. If you do not call or raise a bet, you must fold your hand.

Four-flush: Any four cards to a flush. If you have two hearts in the pocket and see two more hearts on the flop, you have a four-flush.

Four-of-a-kind: Four cards of the same value, such as four aces.

Fourth Street: The second to last of the five community cards; the first card to hit the board after the flop; also known as "the turn."

Free card: Usually associated with the last two betting rounds—if all players check, the dealer turns over a "free" card. There were no bets to call, so the card did not "cost" the players.

Full house: Three-of-a-kind and a pair.

Garbage: A hand with no pair or better. Most often, such a hand is void of any high card. If you haven't seen garbage before, this is what it looks like: 3-5-9-2-7 (off-suit, of course).

Gimmick: You don't hear the term very much anymore, but if you do, look out! It means that a player is using a cheating method to win. A common term for a player using a gimmick is *mechanic*. Yes, it still happens, even in the better poker rooms. Incidentally, a mechanic could also be a dealer, but that's so unlikely in today's highly regulated casinos, particularly the major resort casinos and poker clubs. The theory, however, is that a dealer could be working in collusion with a player to help ensure a big win, and then later sharing in the profits.

Giving your hand away: A more common way to say it is "tipping your hand," but it doesn't necessarily mean literally showing another player your cards; the term refers to some careless action, or words spoken, on the part of a player that "gives your hand away." A good rule to follow is to use an economy of words at the poker tables.

Grifter: (1) A cheat. (2) A person without formal education (exhibiting low intellect), yet successful in spite of these shortcomings.

Hand: This simple word has multiple meanings. (1) Your held cards. (2) The best five-card ranking you can make from your pocket cards and community cards. (3) From start to completion of all the betting rounds. "I'm going to stay in for one more hand." (4) Synonymous with "game." (Casino personnel use the term *game* to mean one betting event.)

Heads up: (1) A game with only two players. (2) A hand that is down to two players. Another term for "heads up" is "one-on-one."

Hole cards: In Hold 'em, the hole cards are the two pocket cards dealt face down to each player. In any poker game, a hole card is a card unseen by other players. Similar terms are *down* and *under*. "He had aces in the hole." "He had aces under." "He had aces down."

In the money: A player in a tournament is said to be "in the money" when he or she makes it to the final table, where all nine positions win a portion of the "purse." In some cases, a "money position" can occur before the final table; in other cases, not all players at the final table win a share of the prize money.

Inside straight: A hand with four cards to a straight, usually needing an "interior" card to fill, such as 3-4-5-7. The interior card needed to make the straight is a 6. Since an inside straight suggests that only one card is needed to fill, that needed card could also be on the end of only two possible 4-to-a-straight hands: J-Q-K-A and A-2-3-4. The term *inside straight* is often used with the verb *draw:* "He's drawing to an "inside straight."

Jackpot: A casino promotion offering prize money for selected high hands or other rare occurrences. As an example, a particular "bad beat" (losing a high hand to an even higher hand) could be a prize winner. Some jackpots are "progressive," meaning that the amount to win is continually increasing until a winner is declared.

Kicker: In Hold 'em, a high card in your hand that may be needed to break tie hands of less than five cards. "They both had a pair of 10s, but Jim's ace kicker won the pot."

Ladies: Poker jargon for "queens." Generally, the term is reserved for a pair.

Late position: One of the last three betting positions (the player on the button, and the two players to the right of the button). In late position, a player has a distinct advantage because other players have already acted on their hands.

Laydown: Another term for "fold," although "laydown" is generally used in later betting rounds when a player folds a decent hand in fear of another player's developing hand that could be stronger.

Limit: In a limit game, bets and raises are restricted to specific amounts. For example, in a $2-$4 game, all bets and raises during the first two rounds must be $2. All bets and raises during the final two rounds must be $4.

Limp in: A term only occasionally heard to mean simply calling the "big blind." If no other players called, the big blind wins the small blind. "He limped in to see the flop."

Live hand: A player has a live hand until folded or lost. Occasionally, players need to be reminded that it's their turn, forgetting they had a live hand.

Lock: Holding the best possible hand; synonymous with the term *nuts*.

Low stakes: A term that means different limits to different players. Clearly, a $2-$4 game is low stakes. But is a $10-$20 game low stakes, too? For some; not for others.

Muck: Another term for "fold," and for the discard pile.

No limit: A Hold 'em game with no prearranged betting structure. In No-Limit Hold 'em, players can wager up to the full amount they have in front of them.

Nuts: You have "the nuts" if you have a hand that no one can beat. Same as "lock." Say the board shows A-9-8-K-5 with no more than two cards suited (ruling out a flush). If you hold a 6-7, you've made your straight and nobody can beat you since no higher straight is possible and the next highest hand is a full house. Without a pair on the board, there is no chance for a full house.

Off-suit: Cards of different suits, such as jack of clubs and king of diamonds.

On the end: The river card; the last card dealt to the board.

Open-ended straight: A hand of 4-to-a-straight, whereby one of two cards can make the straight. In the more typical case, the four cards held are consecutive and do not include an ace. With a hand of 5-6-7-8, either a 4 or a 9 will make the straight. Many players overlook such a hand as 4-6-7-8-10. It is also an open-ended straight, in the sense that one of two cards can make the straight, even though both cards are "interior cards," not "end" cards. The straight can be made 4-5-6-7-8, or 6-7-8-9-10.

Outs: The number of cards yet to be seen that can improve your hand. If you are holding an open-ended straight, and none of the cards on the board can fill it for you, you have eight outs, assuming there's at least one inning, uh, betting round to go.

Overcard: A card on the board that is higher than either of your pocket cards, suggesting that another player could have at least a pair that could beat you, even if you pair up one of your pocket cards in a later draw.

Paint: The face cards: jack, queen, and king.

Pocket cards: The two cards dealt (face down) to a player; also known as "hole" cards.

Pocket pair: If both "pocket" cards are of the same value, such as two jacks, you have a "pocket pair."

Post: To put in the ante or blinds prior to the deal of the cards.

Pot limit: A limit set on any bet or raise based on the amount of money in the pot at that time. Pot limit is the least common among the three accepted forms of betting structure. The other two are simply "limit," and "no limit."

Rack: A plastic tray used to carry your chips from the cashier to the table. A rack holds five stacks of 20 chips. Incidentally, never play "out of the rack." When you get to the table, remove the chips and stack them in front of you.

Rake: The amount of money drawn from each pot by the casino dealer, either a fixed amount or a percentage, that serves as the casino's profit for running the game.

Rebuy: A player's option during a tournament to buy more chips. Usually one rebuy is allowed within a certain time frame. Many tournaments do not offer rebuys.

River: The last community card dealt. Also known as fifth street.

Rock: A player who only stays in with strong pocket cards and, even then, exhibits overly conservative play. "Rocks" do not particularly like tournaments where the blinds are continually raised, because if you don't bet very often, the blinds will eat up your chips.

Roll: (1) To turn a card or cards face up. An old term, but still in use today. (2) A shortened form of the word *bankroll*.

Royal flush: The highest poker hand in Hold 'em. A-K-Q-J-10 of the same suit. Also known as an ace-high straight flush. Since there are only five community cards and only two pocket cards, it's impossible that two players could hold a royal flush at the same time.

Satellite: A Hold 'em tournament designed primarily as a means of entry to a larger tournament. The cost of entry is minimal compared to the major tournament you would like to enter.

Set: A poker hand of three-of-a-kind in which two of the three cards are pocket cards (hole cards) and the other card of the set is a community card (on the board). It is incorrect to refer to any three-of-a-kind as a "set." Since two of the three cards are hidden, a "set" is usually a strong, deceptive hand.

Shootout: A tournament where there is no consolidation of tables, and a winner is decided from each table. These winners proceed to another table (or tables) until only one winner remains at a final table holding all the marbles. Shootouts give a player the opportunity to play against a full table, then progressively fewer players, down to a one-on-one confrontation. Since poker strategy changes as the number of players change, a shootout is a truer test of the players' abilities by forcing them to continually alter their strategies.

Short-handed: A Hold 'em game with fewer than five players.

Showdown: A comparison of the full hands of all active players at the end of the final betting round to determine the winner of the pot.

Slow-playing: A deceptive playing strategy whereby a player has a strong hand yet plays it as if it's a weak hand by checking or just calling bets. The purpose of this strategy is to pull out bigger bets on later betting rounds. It should be noted that this tactic can often backfire. A similar term is *sandbagging*.

Slow-roller: A player who holds the winning hand, yet, through facial expressions and mannerisms, let's another player think that he or she has won the pot. Then, just as that player reaches for the chips, the slow-roller shows the winning hand, usually with a smirky smile. Few poker players have the patience for this kind of childish behavior.

Small blind: (1) A forced bet (to ensure action) made by the player who is one position left of the dealer button. The small blind is posted (made) before any cards are dealt. In limit games, the amount of this bet is usually one-half of the big blind. (2) The term may also refer to the player who is in that position.

Soft-playing: A play made for the benefit of another player or players; typically seen when close friends or relatives are playing at the same table. It's not uncommon for some players to soft-play (go easy) on players who are down on their luck. It should be noted, however, that this sometimes altruistic act is not fair to other players who are not on the receiving end of such generosity. A commonly heard excuse is that a soft play was unintentional. Still, many poker players will bow out of a table if they find out or suspect that two or more players are close relatives. No one wants to play against a team.

Spot-card: Any card other than a face card or ace. Count the spots and use the old poker players' jargon: a 4-spot, a 5-spot, and so on.

Spread: To show your hand at the "showdown."

Square-up: A responsibility of dealers to ensure that each player has equal and sufficient room to play. Most Hold 'em tables will seat 10 or 11 players, but—many players will agree—only 9 players *comfortably*. If you believe that an adjacent player is moving in on your space, ask the dealer to square-up the table.

Standoff: Two identical high hands that share the pot equally.

Stealing the blinds: The act of raising on the first round of betting in the hope of making all the other players fold, and you win the blinds.

Straight: Five cards in consecutive order, not all of the same suit. If they are all suited (the same suit), the hand is called a "straight flush."

Suited: Cards of the same suit, such as jack and king of spades.

Sympathy show: At a showdown, a player with a losing hand shows it because it was a strong hand.

Table stakes: A limit set on a game whereby players can bet only what's "on the table." You can't go into your pocket for more ammo. At least that's the rule in a casino-run game. In a hotel-room game, you can probably bet your Rolex! If that's not enough, there's always that deed to the lost gold mine.

Tell: A motion, a twitch, a nervous habit—however subtle—broadcast by a player for other players to read. The idea is that tells can signal the strength, or weakness, of the subject player's hand. A tell can be as simple as a raised eyebrow, or as complicated as a series or pattern of glances.

Toke: Also called a "tip" or "gratuity," it's given to a dealer by any player, not necessarily a winner. Tips can become a significant drain on some players who simply go overboard with their gratuities. Players may unknowingly "double-tip" in cases where a percentage of the pot is automatically held out for the dealer. There is no rule that says you must tip a dealer, but it is common courtesy to do so, especially if you're a winner and the dealer has been friendly and courteous. Just remember to tip in moderation.

Trips: Poker slang, short for "triplets." If you have "trips," you have 3-of-a-kind.

Turn: The first community card dealt after the flop. Also known as Fourth Street.

Winner Take All: A tournament concept whereby the sole winner either wins all the chips or wins the announced prize. There is no prize distribution for second-place, third-place and so-on finishes. This form of tournament is disliked by a multitude of players, and, accordingly, does not usually draw well.

Woolworth: Of all the old poker jargon, little of which is used today, this one is still a popular favorite. If you have a "Woolworth," you've got a pair of 5s and a pair of 10s. That's right, five and dime.

World Series Of Poker: The mother lode of all poker tournaments, held each summer at the Rio Hotel and Casino in Las Vegas.

CHAPTER 7

A WINNER'S NOTEBOOK

Let me tell you what I do, and what I *don't* do, as part of a general plan I follow when I gamble, regardless of the game. A few of these important points have been covered earlier, but allow me to give them to you again in a more organized fashion. Besides, picking up on my advice a second time can only help you in your pursuit of victory.

WHAT I DO

1. I always watch a game before I play. My "stakeout" might end up with a walk. In fact, most often it does. This is the time to let your intuitive senses take charge.

2. I think of my play in terms of sessions, which are usually short. Again, the idea is to strike quickly and run. Obviously, I don't "run" as long as the dealer is putting chips in front of me. I run when an opportunity has ended.

3. I start each session with the same modest stake, and always begin with wagers at the table-minimum level. My starting stake for each session is forty dollars (two twenty-dollar bills). Never any more; never any less. It's a discipline that has saved me from ruin more times than you could imagine.

4. I follow a betting progression designed to ensure that I won't miss out on a fabulous streak of wins. In years past, I had missed out on numerous opportunities and vowed that I would never let it happen again. My incremental betting habits have forced me to ride these waves when they roll in. And you know what? Practicing this strategy has taught me more than just taking advantage of rare betting opportunities; it has taught me how to spot them early, and jump on before other players can sense what's happening. More on this later.

5. I exit a session when one of two triggers kicks in: I lose two bets in a row, or my stake dwindles to 50 percent of its value. That's right. I not only know how to quit winners, I know how to quit losers, too. Just as it's important to maximize your winnings, it's equally important to minimize losses. There are two points worth noting from this important discipline: (1) I will always walk away with at least a significant portion of my original stake, and (2) I will never lose three bets in a row at the same table.*

*The author has published details of his betting strategies in other books. His first strategy, and perhaps the most effective, is called the "Gollehon Betting Strategy" and is found in his bestselling book, *What Casinos Don't Want You To Know*. His "Simplified Four-Color Strategy," a shortened version of this book's "Power Progressive Strategy," can be found in his book, *Casino Gambling*. A third strategy, geared to craps players, is called "Power Betting" and can be found in his book, *Conquering Casino Craps*.

6. I take frequent breaks. The strict exit rules I follow force me to do this. Breaks give me time to cash in chips, making sure I have those two twenties to start my next assault. Breaks from the action can be anything from a stop in the coffee shop to a leisurely walk outdoors. My breaks, incidentally, are not short. Nor do they bore me.I always enjoy the anticipation of my next session.

WHAT I DON'T DO

1. I'm not a grind player. I don't commandeer a spot at a table and stay there for hours on end. I'm not there to play. I'm there to win! Never get too comfy at the tables. Forget the idea of "settling in." I remember watching a guy peel off ten C-notes and turn them into ten grand in ten minutes. Boy, did he hit 'em quickly! But he didn't leave, he stuck around. Before I left the table, I remember his asking the dealers if he would have any trouble cashing in his high-denomination chips. It was a small, out-of-the-way Indian casino, and, I guess, he was afraid he might get hassled. When I saw him at that same table an hour or so later, he had given back at least half of his win. Later in the day I saw him there again, with nothing but a few piddling chips in front of him. He had worried for nothing.

2. I never play for comps. Frankly, I don't like the idea of casino bosses even knowing who I am. Comps tend to make players feel a little too cozy with the casino, as if they have established a warm, sporting relationship. You do this for me, I'll do this for you. Play at this level for this much time, and you'll get this much back in comp rewards. No thank you. I don't want the casino to influence the way I play. Besides, I table-hop so often, because of my frequent breaks, that it would be nearly impossible for a casino boss to keep a tab on my play. Understand this: Comps are a casino's most effective trap to lure players into deeper waters than they want to go.

3. I don't set limits on my winnings, although I do set limits on my losses. It's a point of contention among gaming writers, but I don't see how there can be any dispute. If you're winning, keep playing! And play hard.

Winning sessions are not the rule, they are the exception. Learn how to take full advantage.

4. I don't look down my nose at a token win. Hey, a win is a win. Be happy with it. Even if it's only a few dollars, take it and be thankful. A win beats a loss every time. If you're going to be greedy about it, settling for only large wins, heed one of my favorite gambling maxims: Greed turns winners into losers. Astute gamblers have learned how to take what they can get.

5. I don't linger. When it's time for me to leave, I leave. And no one knows this better than my wife, Kathy. We leave so expeditiously, you'd think the place was on fire! After a full slate of sessions, whether I've won or lost, I know the importance of a quick exit. It's my way of avoiding the temptation to go back for more, or worse, to try to get even. It might sound like a Yogiism, but I consider it one of my top tips: When it's over, it's over. Most gamblers just haven't learned how to pack it up.

WORTH REMEMBERING

1. I temper my anxiety to gamble. I always schedule something else to do upon my arrival… a lunch, a meeting, a dip in the pool.

2. I think positive! Casinos are full of negative people and negative situations. I avoid them like the plague.

3. I always have my intuition switch turned on. It could be the most powerful weapon we have. Few people use it.

4. I leave three things at home: superstitions, systems, and revenge. The first two are obvious. In the third case, I never think of a casino as owing me anything!

5. I shop for the best games. There *are* differences!

6. I never play to impress. Big bets won't make me a better player. Big bets won't change the cards.

7. I never play on credit. Easy come, easy go.

8. I know when to be aggressive, and when not to. I switch gears often, although mostly I'm riding in my conservative mode.

9. I take with me precisely the right bankroll for a particular trip. No more; no less.

10. I never play the newer casino games. They are designed as rapid-decision affairs with no skill to speak of and fraught with percentages that are too high for me to consider.

11. I never play if I'm tired or moody or have too many things on my mind.

12. I never bet against a trend. Always bet *with* a streak, never against it.

13. I make gambling a planned destination trip. I never go gambling on a whim.

14. I never play on weekends or holidays. Only on weekdays. I have more choices and more space.

15. I always focus on my only objective: TO WIN!

MOST EXCITING BETS:

1. Horse Racing
2. Craps
3. Sports

SMARTEST BETS:

1. At a blackjack table, a double down on 11 with the dealer showing 6, especially if your count shows a great excess of 10-value cards!

2. The odds bet on both pass-line and come bets at a craps table (particularly 5X and 10X odds).

3. A 7-9 or better video poker machine (7 coins for a flush, 9 coins for a full house).

DUMBEST BETS:

1. Keno. The more numbers you mark, the dumber the bet!

2. The 5-number bet at the roulette table costs you 7.89 percent; all other bets are 5.26 percent. Hardly a bargain.

3. One-roll bets at the craps table, especially "any 7"—a whopping 16.67 percent!

SMARTEST MOVES:

1. Counting cards at blackjack (no continuous shuffler).

2. Developing psychological skills for the poker tables.

3. Clocking a "single zero" roulette wheel.

DUMBEST MOVES:

1. Never hitting a stiff at a blackjack table.

2. Tracking previous numbers at a roulette wheel.

3. Playing a nickel slot machine that requires more than 5 coins to "play the max."

SKILL GAMES:

1. Poker
2. Horse Racing
3. Sports Betting

The classic skill game is poker, but horse racing and sports betting are certainly skill oriented, too. You should know, however, that handicapping horses and sports teams requires a tremendous amount of study and research to be successful over the long term.

Video poker and craps have certain skills associated with them, too, but these skills are rarely enough to overcome a narrow house edge. The games are more correctly called *low-percentage games*.

Although this book's title suggests that the games we've covered are vulnerable to the casino, it should be noted that Texas Hold 'em and other poker games are not really won or lost at the expense of a casino, but at the expense of the players, particularly weak, unskilled players. Casinos routinely take a percentage of pots in limit games and a percentage of the buy-ins in no-limit games. They really don't care who wins or loses.

Blackjack can no longer be considered a true skill game because of so many recent rule changes and casino countermeasures, not to mention the widespread installation of continuous shufflers. It is, however, a strong low-percentage game that, under the right conditions, can produce an unusual frequency of wins.

For the great majority of players, however, even the bona fide skill games should be considered only as low-percentage games because the element of skill (and discipline) is rarely played to its fullest. But for those few who do, it's money in the bank!

TRAITS OF A PROFESSIONAL POKER PLAYER

When I created this list, the idea going in was to find the raw qualities that seem to define the top players. But the more I looked at it, the list defined a good gambler in general, not just poker players. The listing is in no particular order. See how many of these traits *you* have.

Passion	Tenacity	Stamina
Courage	Persistence	Experience
Dedication	Focus	Logic
Knowledge	Discipline	Perception

TRAITS OF A ROOKIE PLAYER

Here's a short list of traits that usually work against you in a casino. They help you lose. In fact, these dubious traits may be worth losing altogether.

Ego	Anxiety	Superstition
Greed	Fear	Desperation

IF DAVE CAN DO IT...

I started this book with a story about a player who gave up his video-poker winnings so that he could have his "fun" at the dice tables. Remember?

If you read that story, you learned from it because losing is the great teacher. But winning can teach too, so allow me to end this book with a story about a winner. You'll learn from it too.

Dave Friedman moved to Las Vegas several years ago after quitting his job as a mid-level manager. My old golfing buddy wanted to see if his incredible skill in rating college football teams could turn into a means of making a living. He wanted to gamble legally; he wisely chose Vegas.

I know this guy inside and out. He's a research freak. Put him in a library, spread books all over the table in front of him, and he's in his element. The boon of the Internet has been a blessing for this guy. He navigates the net like Columbus sailed the ocean blue. But newspapers and magazines—sports magazines, of course—are still his bread-and-butter sources.

It's worth noting the way he watches a game. He doesn't do it like you and I do. He tapes every game he can and studies the plays as if he were one of the coaches of the teams. He has a remarkable sense about him of figuring out at exactly what level a team will play based on games earlier in the season or, to some extent, the past season. He thinks it's the Number One factor in sports handicapping: Ranking teams in terms of emotion, desire, and toughness. Not overall, of course, but specifically for the upcoming weekend. A team that crushes a tough opponent one week might be low on his list for the following week. And if you ask him why, he'll give you an hour's worth of reasons.

Anyhow. Let me cut to the chase. Dave has been in Vegas now for about three years. Here's his track record. The first year he was a little nervous, and a little too conservative. He made about $25,000 net of expenses. And, yes... he reported all of it as income. He treated his venture as a business, setting up a plush office in one of his bedrooms at home. His record-keeping would knock you over. He hired a bookkeeper to help keep him organized (his only shortfall)... keep the books, and pay the taxes.

The second year was better. He cleared about $75,000. The third year was the charm. Over a quarter-of-a-million dollars!

THE VALUE OF "ALERTS"

Whether at the poker tables, at the racetrack, or in the sportsbooks, I keep two sets of alerts that I always refer to. Safely tucked in my wallet, these alerts, or signals, or whatever you want to call them, are always on, always there to alert me to a situation that can either make me vulnerable or make me a winner. One set is basic to all forms of gambling; the other sets are unique to a particular game. Start thinking about things that you believe belong on *your* list.

MANAGING MONEY

I suggest you top your basic alert list with the same one that's on top of mine. After all, the very idea of keeping your winnings—as obvious as that might sound— should be front and center on every gambler's agenda. Whenever you feel an unwarranted urge to spend a goodly portion of your winnings, you should hear the alert. Is it time to leave the tables, to walk away from the track?

The way I manage my money is two-fold: First, I play off my bankroll in strict limits per game, session, or day, depending on whether I'm betting poker, horses, or sports. It's a basic tenet of money management called "budgeting." All players say they do it; most players don't.

Second, I keep my bankroll... and my winnings, separate. In many cases, particularly if there is considerable money at issue, I'll put my winnings in a safe-deposit box that most all casinos provide today. If I'm at a racetrack, I'll often ask that a big winning ticket is paid by check. For those of you who try to hide your winnings from the feds, you'll probably get a W2-G issued by the track, so what's the point? Besides, if you're going to hide your winnings, I'd rather see you hide it from crooks, or, for that matter, from yourself! Who could do the most damage to your winnings… you, crooks, or a good tax account? Think about it.

HOUSE MONEY

It's a term that can only get you into trouble. The phrase is part of an old cliché among gamblers that I'm sure you've heard: "I'm betting with house money." The expression sprang up in the sportsbooks many years ago before the term "house money" was inserted for "the bookie's money." In fact, sports bettors are still the biggest victim of this charade, but I hear it around the track and in the poker rooms, too. So listen up: **When the money's in your pocket, it's your money!**

What difference does it make how it got there? Are your winnings a different color than your original stake? Are you applying two different values to money? I think so. And I think that this kind of attitude can only lead to reckless, senseless losses. Remember, when the money's in your pocket, it's your money! If you think of it as house money, the house will eventually get it back.

It's just another example of thinking the way the casino wants you to think.

WINNER'S MAXIMS

I don't feel that driving urge to play that most people do. I don't have an urge to play; I have an urge to win! And for me, patience almost always helps me find it.

I firmly believe that what separates winners from losers is much more than luck, and even much more than skill. It's an uncanny ability to just know when. When to jump on it, when to ease back, and when to walk.

The gambler who tells everyone else how to play is always the one who wins the least.

Players who give worthy advice are wasting their time. Good players don't need it, and fools won't heed it.

There are few players who really catch my attention anymore. But occasionally I'll see a player, usually at a craps table, who can scare the dots off the dice. There's nothing wrong with being aggressive. It's how fortunes are made. The key, of course, is timing. Aggressive players are cunning and patient. They know when to strike, and they strike hard.

For gamblers, there are no sure things. There are no impossible things. And everything in between is just a matter of odds.

You'll never win big if you don't know how to win small.

Most casino players think they're experts. An expert is a guy who knows 47 ways to make love, but can't find a girlfriend.

In the casino, you must have the ability to recognize an opportunity, the wisdom to know that you can't force it to happen, and the discipline to quit when it's gone.

All players love to win money; there are a few players who just love to win.

Overheard in a casino: "We didn't win anything; we only lost a few hundred dollars; but we had fun!" Whoa! Don't ever let your gambling reach the point where losing is fun!

I simply don't subscribe to silly superstitions, but I do wholeheartedly believe in my instincts. When I gamble, I take along my most trusted friend. I never gamble with a fool.

Having a lot of money is never a reason to bet a lot of money.

Winning is one thing; keeping it is another.

If you win, and you're not excited, then you haven't won at all.

Earlier in this closing chapter, I listed the three most exciting bets and topped that list with horse racing. For those of you who would argue that horse racing provides the most exciting win, I have a backup answer, perhaps a better one: What's the most exciting bet you can make? You got it!

A bet that wins!

Here's how to get your own set of John Gollehon's personal Strategy Cards and save MONEY doing it!

The author's popular Strategy Cards have become the hottest cards on the market! The set retails for $12 in shops, but you can order the complete set by mail for only $9.95. Your cards go out within 48 hours and we pay the first-class postage!

BLACKJACK: Every player-hand and dealer up-card combination is listed, so you'll know exactly when to hit, stand, split, or double down. The Strategy Card does all the work!

CRAPS: All the payoffs for the bets you'll be making are listed so you can be sure you're getting all the winnings you deserve! A complete rundown for playing the game is also included.

VIDEO POKER: Follow a clever strategy to increase your chances of hitting a royal flush by 20 percent! The best paytables are listed, so you'll know exactly what machines to look for.

ROULETTE: A precise layout of the wheel is shown so that you can clock the dealer and predict the segment where the ball should land. See if you can beat the wheel with skill!

HOW TO ORDER:

Send check or money order for only $9.95 to: Gollehon Press, Inc., 6157 28th St. SE, Grand Rapids, MI 49546. Just write "Strategy Cards" on a piece of paper along with your name and address printed neatly.

Order your complete set today and start winning!